Group's

Sticky
Faith

52 family messages for big church

Group

Loveland, Colorado
group.com

Group resources actually work!

This Group resource incorporates our R.E.A.L. approach to ministry. It reinforces a growing friendship with Jesus, encourages long-term learning, and results in life transformation, because it's

Relational
Learner-to-learner interaction enhances learning and builds Christian friendships.

Experiential
What learners experience through discussion and action sticks with them up to 9 times longer than what they simply hear or read.

Applicable
The aim of Christian education is to equip learners to be both hearers and doers of God's Word.

Learner-based
Learners understand and retain more when the learning process takes into consideration how they learn best.

Visit our website: **group.com**

Credits
Chief Creative Officer: Joani Schultz
Authors: Jody Brolsma, Mikal Keefer, Gina Leuthauser
Senior Editor: Jan Kershner
Senior Developer, Children's Ministry: Patty Smith
Children's Ministry Champion: Christine Yount Jones
Copy Editor: Dena Twinem
Art Director: Andrea Filer
Print Production Artist: YaYe Design
Cover Art Director: Andrea Filer
Cover Designer: The Designworks Group
Production Manager: DeAnne Lear
Senior Project Manager: Pam Clifford

Unless otherwise indicated, all Scripture quotations are taken from the *Holy Bible*, New Living Translation, copyright © 1996, 2004. Used by permission of Tyndale House Publishers, Inc., Carol Stream, Illinois 60188. All rights reserved.

Library of Congress Cataloging-in-Publication Data
Sticky faith : 52 family messages for big church.
    p. cm.
ISBN 978-0-7644-3711-3 (pbk. : alk. paper)
1. Church work with families. 2. Family--Religious life. 3. Big churches. I. Group Publishing.
BV4438.S75 2009
268'.432--dc22
                                        2008031772

ISBN 0-7644-3711-3

10 9 8 7 6 5 4 3 2 1   18 17 16 15 14 13 12 11 10 09

Printed in the United States of America.

Contents

Old Testament

New Testament

Introduction

Sticky faith.

It's what we all want—for our church, for ourselves, and for our kids. Faith that sticks. Faith that stays with us after we leave the church walls. Faith that helps us know what to say and how to act. Faith that propels us to tell our friends why we love Jesus.

But how can you begin to instill such faith when your audience is made up of people of all ages, from 5 to 85? How can you reach them all in one simple message?

This book can help! You'll find 52 interactive messages where adults and kids share an experience in big church. Each 3-5 minute experience engages kids and adults so they grow in faith together. Use them anytime during your regular service or message. They're that versatile!

But the faith-building doesn't stop there. *Sticky Faith* comes with an enhanced CD-ROM that contains 52 printable bulletin inserts that tie to each interactive message. These inserts, called Sticky Notes, help families take their faith home and put it to use in everyday life—at home, in the car, anywhere.

You'll create simple, engaging experiences during big church where adults and kids can learn and grow together in fun, meaningful ways.

So what are you waiting for? Turn the page and start sticking!

You'll see this symbol each time food is used. Please read this tip carefully.

Allergy Alert!

Some of the projects in this book involve food. Be aware that some children have food allergies that can be dangerous. Know your children, and consult with parents about allergies their children may have. Also be sure to carefully read food labels, as hidden ingredients can cause allergy-related problems.

Clueless:
Confessions of a Preaching Pastor

As lead pastor of a Colorado church, Kent Hummel knows his way around a pulpit. He's been in the ministry 30 years, moving from youth ministry into a senior pastor role. He's an accomplished teacher and preacher.

And—he was quick to discover a few years ago—pretty much clueless about connecting with children from the pulpit.

"That wasn't part of my training in seminary," says Kent. "It wasn't part of my direct ministry experience. There were things I didn't know...and I didn't know I didn't know them."

At Kent's church the children's ministry team takes off the month of August. Other than the nursery, all Sunday school classes are suspended so volunteers can enjoy worship together with their families.

Which means children are seated with parents in "Big People's Church."

It seemed like a good idea at the time

Because Kent knew there would be hundreds of children in his audience during the month of August, Kent decided to tackle the Ten Commandments.

"It seemed like material that could include kids," says Kent. "I still think so. But I quickly got feedback that maybe I'd gone about delivering it the wrong way."

Indeed.

Before the start of the first week's sermon, Kent asked the children to come forward and be seated on the floor. He announced that any child who memorized the Ten Commandments and was able to recite them after the final Sunday in August would receive a $10 bill.

The children *loved* the idea—but some of the children's ministry team was less enthused.

"Three things immediately happened," says Mikal Keefer, a volunteer in the church's children's ministry.

"First, our regular Bible memory program took a torpedo beneath the waterline. We had prizes to celebrate when children memorized verses, but nothing like $10 bills. The motivation for children to memorize became a paycheck—and that shifted motivation from intrinsic to extrinsic. The program faltered.

"Second, kids whose families had been planning vacations during that last week of August faced full-scale revolt. No child wanted to miss the chance to recite.

"And third, it was obvious that while this program would appear to be successful—kids would memorize a section of the phone book or the Koran for 10 dollars—it would all be short-term learning. There was no application, no follow-through.

"Kent hadn't intended any of those results. He was trying to be inclusive and encouraging, to build involvement.

"But there *was* a better way."

A meeting of the minds

Shortly after August, Kent was approached about adopting a new strategy for the next August. He enthusiastically welcomed suggestions and soon was meeting with one of the children's ministry team to develop a new approach.

"I'm able to admit when I need help," says Kent. "Preaching in a way that reaches children is most definitely an area where help was needed."

The following August the sermons were about the kingdom parables of Jesus—challenging stuff—and yet children still made the connections. Together, Kent and his children's ministry team had found a way to engage children without losing the adult audience.

Even better, families who were seated together in church got to interact together, giving families something to talk about on the way home.

"What made this work was getting children's ministry people involved in the planning," says Kent. "I'm good at helping adults 'get it' in sermons, but I was clueless about connecting with kids.

"Our children's ministry people think in ways I don't, and it's a huge advantage to do planning with people who understand the children's segment of our audience."

Lasting benefits

Kent reports that the August experience has impacted his preaching to adults, too.

"It opened my eyes to thinking about variety. How can I make a point in several ways, through different learning styles? That's a question I wasn't asking before, and now I see more engagement throughout the congregation when I preach."

Kent is also more careful to avoid language that might be easily misunderstood. "That's something I had to do when children were present, and it's a good idea to do for adults, as well."

He's quick to define terms, and give examples, to make certain he's communicating clearly and being understood.

"The thing is," says Kent, "all the things that make sermons more effective for children make them more effective for adults, too."

Is your teaching pastor uncertain if it's worthwhile trying to connect with kids? Share this article!

How to connect with kids... without losing adults along the way

Sunday morning. You look out at a congregation that includes both adults *and* children. You want your message to be meaningful to the adults but still engage the children.

How exactly can you make *that* happen?

Here's what *not* to do: Don't write a message for adults and then "dumb it down" so children can grasp what you're saying. Using shorter words, tossing in references to childhood situations, and sharing a story from your childhood won't do the trick.

Try that and you'll not only fail to connect with kids—you'll lose your adult audience, too.

The good news: You *can* connect with children and still hang on to the adults in your audience.

The bad news: It takes work—and planning. But it's worth the effort.

Following are 10 things to keep in mind as you craft a sermon or message that's meaningful for both children and adults. If you take care of all these issues, you'll look out at a congregation that's actively listening, participating, and growing in their faith—both adults *and* kids.

1. Pick the right topic and text

Remember: Children tend to think in concrete, real-world terms until they reach upper-elementary age. They're bright and quick to understand; they're just not wired like adults.

Which means children will track with you better if you're talking about a significant event in Scripture rather than a theological concept. Children are still becoming biblically literate; they need to know about the personalities and role models in Scripture.

But don't worry about offending the adults in your audience; most of *them* need to become biblically literate, too.

Children are also easily confused when you use "churchy" language and metaphors. Tell adults that "Jesus is in your heart" and you communicate you have a vibrant, heartfelt relationship with Christ.

Say the same thing to a child and she'll wonder how Jesus got in there...and whether you swallowed him or he tunneled in through your navel.

2. Stick with one point—and approach it from different directions

Some adults *love* teachings loaded with cross-references and in-depth observations. These footnote-lovers are *not* children.

The typical sermon has three points...which is two too many for children. And, truth be told, it's two too many for most adults.

Children do best with "one point" learning—having the entire lesson focused on *one significant point*. Each activity and illustration reinforces that one point. All roads lead there.

So pick one point. Say it often—five or six times isn't too many. And be sure that no matter where your message takes you, it quickly makes a beeline back to that point.

3. Start with a "Wow!"

Children are just like grown-ups: They're easily distracted. If you want to have their attention, you need to capture it—and that's best done by starting with something unexpected.

The 52 activities you'll find in this book provide ready-to-go "Wows" for you to use, but preach long enough and you'll need to create your own attention-grabbing introductions.

Here's an example of how to create one...

Suppose you're teaching about Jesus' parable of the lost coin. Consider what you might do other than stand up and start talking. Something that elicits emotion and requires active involvement.

So rather than just talking, walk over to where the offering plates sit and start pawing desperately through the offerings. Insist, with panic in your voice, that there's a very special coin that's supposed to be there—but it's missing.

Enlist the congregation's help finding that special coin (a Sacagawea dollar would work nicely, or a foreign coin). Proclaim loudly that it's in the sanctuary, maybe taped under a pew. Not until the coin is found can you continue.

The fact you're touching the offering (sacrilege!) will get attention. That you ask the help of the congregation prompts emotion and demands participation and focus—a "Wow!" that pulls everyone onto the same page of caring about a lost coin. Just like the woman in the parable.

4. Engage emotion

Most sermons are emotionally boring. That is, they may engage an audience intellectually but they seldom elicit an *emotional* response.

More than one study confirms that information connected with emotion is far likelier to "stick" than information that's presented without emotion. If we want what we say to leave an impact, we've got to build emotion into our messages.

How? Well, consider our example of looking for the coin. It puts audience members in the uncomfortable position of having to decide if they'll help. They're curious as to why the coin is so important. They're possibly irritated that they're expected to paw around under a pew where they might find a splinter or ancient wad of gum.

Any of those emotions is fine—they all work. Do avoid evoking rage or jealousy, but a minor negative emotional response still throws open the doors of long-term memory and deeper learning.

5. Get everyone involved

And that means *everyone*. Your goal is to, at some point of your message, have everyone in the room actively participating. It can be a discussion...by doing parts of a drama (putting the majority of the audience in the role of "sound effects" is a legitimate way to involve them)...or all voting for or against something.

Involvement is something children crave—and adults embrace if it's presented as safe and fun. Be clear about what involvement you want, and demonstrate it. Children are quicker to jump in than their parents, but if the loss of dignity isn't too severe, adults will hop on the bandwagon, too.

6. Be visual...and auditory...and musical...and...

Most sermons are all about words. And many children (and adults) love a good story.

But not *everyone* loves stories.

We all learn differently, so be careful to include as many learning styles as possible in your introduction and sermon. Eight learning styles are listed at the end of this introduction as a quick reference guide.

7. Switch it up

Rule of thumb: Every four to six minutes, shift directions. Move to an activity. Invite people to turn to a neighbor and talk. Sing a song. Stop to reflect. Show a video clip. Change *something*—it keeps your audience engaged.

Children have an attention span that stretches about one minute for each year of age. A third-grader can hang with you about eight minutes before drifting off. And the maximum for people—of any age—is about 20 minutes.

Making changes is your best way to keep the audience involved.

8. Vary the ebb and flow

A fast activity, a slow one, a loud moment, a quiet one...be intentional about building in variety. Kids love variety and surprise. So do adults.

9. Value relationships

When people learn together, the learning sticks far longer than when we all scuttle off to study on our own. There's something about making learning collaborative that fires up retention...so take advantage of that.

Ask people to talk with each other to make a discovery. To read a passage. To apply a point.

There may be a limited number of things you can do in your sermon setting. But there *are* things you can do. Be inventive!

10. Pray...a lot

It's last on the list but first in importance: Pray.

Pray for wisdom as you consider how to engage others with God's Word and for clarity in hearing God's voice during your preparation.

Pray for patience and perseverance as you hone your message, considering the filters outlined above.

Pray for the people who'll hear you when you speak.

Pray for those who aren't in the audience but need to hear the message.

Pray for yourself—that *you* may be changed by God's Word.

Howard Gardner of Harvard University published a book in 1983 called *Frames of Mind: The Theory of Multiple Intelligences*. The breakthrough notion Gardner espoused was that there are many ways to be smart.

Those ways to be smart are also ways to learn...and if we can tap into all or most of them, we'll "speak the language" of our audience.

Gardner has identified eight intelligences, but suggests there may be more.

Here's the list. But remember: This isn't how children learn best. It's how *people* learn best—children among them. When you address most or all of the learning styles in your teaching or preaching, you intentionally invite everyone in your audience to learn in his or her own preferred style.

Word Smart: These people are big on verbal and linguistic skills. They're good at reading, writing, speaking, storytelling...don't worry too much about connecting with these people. You're sharing a sermon; they're already listening!

Body Smart: These people have great motor skills and are good at dancing, athletics, acting, and using their bodies in other ways. These people need to move; give them a chance during your message. You might have them act something out or pretend to be plants sprouting in the parable of the sower.

Logic/Math Smart: These people are good with numbers, sequencing, analyzing, evaluating, and applying. They love order and tend to avoid chaos. Appeal to logic during your message and these people will hear you loud and clear.

Art/Space Smart: Count on these people to have an eye for detail and color, and to excel in painting, drawing, sculpting, and photography. Can you somehow involve images and pictures in your message? These people will respond.

Music Smart: These people are just as advertised: They gain meaning through music. They may play an instrument or sing, and are sensitive to pitch and rhythm. Connect with these people during your message by allowing them to request a specific song during the worship time.

People Smart: These are "people people." They're sensitive to the feelings, moods, and motives of others. They learn best when they interact with others, which means traditional sermons leave them cold. Work in a time where you ask people to turn to a neighbor to talk. People Smart people will love you.

Self Smart: These are introspective people who are aware of their own feelings, strengths, ideas, values, and beliefs. They set goals. They journal. They like to think and reflect. How can you work in a reflection time for these learners?

Nature Smart: These people have a keen awareness of the natural world. They tend to learn best when the content has to be sorted or classified in relation to the natural world. Drop in a few details when you're talking about the pearl of great price; Nature Smart people will perk right up!

Old Testament

1. A Wonderful Work

The Passage: Genesis 1–2
The Point: You are one of God's amazing creations.
The Props: a 6x9-inch sheet of paper for each person
Quick Summary: You'll use the story of creation to help families discover that they're amazing creations crafted by the hand of God.

Have assistants distribute sheets of paper so each person has one. Then say: **Before God created anything...there was** *nothing*. **Close your eyes to see what "nothing" was like.** Pause for a couple of seconds. **Pretty boring, huh? Open your eyes. First God made light, then he made the sky. I'm going to let** *you* **help me see what else God made. You'll use your paper and tear out the shape of something in creation. I'm going to tell you what to create, but wait until I've given instructions to everyone. This could get noisy!**

Indicate a group of people; for example, "this side of the room" or "folks in the balcony." Before giving the following instructions, point to a specific group. You'll need a total of five groups. Assign one of the following creations to each group:

- plants

- sun, moon, or stars

- fish or birds

- animals

- people

Tip

You can either have assistants distribute the sheets of paper prior to your lesson or include a sheet of paper in each church bulletin.

Allow 30 seconds for kids and adults to make their paper creations. Then draw attention to yourself. Say: **Show your creation to someone sitting nearby, and see if that person can guess what it is.** Pause.

Now discuss the following question:

- **How is your creation like or unlike what God actually created?**

Allow a minute for discussion, then take a few responses from the audience.

Say: **Call out some words that describe** *God's* **creation.** Say the words you hear so everyone can hear them. Then continue: ***You*** **are one of God's creations.** ***You*** **are** (repeat some of the words you heard from the audience).

All too often, we forget that we are God's amazing creations. We live as if our bodies are our own—not the precious and incredible handiwork of God! This week, look at your wobbly, odd-shaped paper creation and then think of the skillful, powerful hands that formed *you*. **And live as one of God's amazing creations.**

Remind everyone to use the fun ideas in the Sticky Note bulletin inserts this week.

2. Chain Reaction

The Passage: Genesis 3

The Point: There are consequences whenever we sin.

The Props: a real domino, or a picture of a domino, for each person

Quick Summary: You'll use the story of Adam and Eve's sin to help families discover that there are *always* consequences when we sin.

Say: **I don't know about you, but I'm kind of warm in here. Let's try an experiment. See if you can cool off someone sitting near you, without touching that person. You've got 30 seconds to try.** Pause while kids and adults cool each other off. People might fan each other with a bulletin or a Bible, or blow on someone's face. Then draw attention to yourself. Ask for a few individuals to share what they did, and repeat the statements for the large group to hear. Ask:

- **What happened when you** (name a few of the actions that people just shared)**?**

Say: **You didn't touch that person, but you made a difference—there was a consequence of your actions. Consequence means the result or effect of an action. You may have cooled someone off, blew air in the person's face, or shared your coffee breath with everyone sitting nearby!**

Say: **I'm sure you've all seen a bunch of dominoes all lined up in a row, right?** Ask:

- **What happens when you push on the first domino?**

Say: **There's a big chain reaction, right? One little touch will knock down one domino, which will knock down the next one, and so on and so on. Well, waving a fan at someone or pushing a domino aren't the only actions with consequences. Let's check out some major consequences in the book of Genesis.**

For Extra Impact

Project a picture of a row of dominoes.

Direct families to open their Bibles to Genesis 3. Say: **Adam and Eve had a perfect place to live. They had a perfect relationship with God.** Hold up one finger. **It only took one little thing to change that.** Read aloud Genesis 3:1-7. Have families discuss this question together:

- **What was the first consequence of sin?**

Say: **That was kind of the first "domino." But it sure wasn't the last. Let's see what else fell down in God's perfect garden.** Read aloud Genesis 3:8-13. Have families discuss this question:

- **What was another result of sin?**

Say: **You can read the rest of Genesis 3 and find many, many more consequences of sin. Like the dominoes, sin kept on rolling. And we still feel the consequences today. Pause for a few seconds and think of a time when your sin affected someone else.** If you feel comfortable, share a time when *your* sin affected others. Be sure what you share is appropriate—and applicable—to kids. For example, you might tell about a time when you got into an argument at school when you were a child and a parent had to come and talk to the principal.

Say: **Even if you think a sin won't hurt anyone else, sin always hurts our relationship with God. Every single time. And that's a consequence God just couldn't bear. That's why he sent Jesus. Jesus took away the worst consequence of our sin—separation from God.**

As you leave today, take a domino with you. Keep it handy as a reminder that our sins *do* affect others. And as a reminder to thank God for sending Jesus to take away our sins.

Have a group of volunteers hand out dominoes as people exit the meeting room. Remind everyone to use the fun ideas in the Sticky Note bulletin inserts this week.

3. Be a Hero

The Passage: Genesis 6:9–8:22
The Point: We can help others stand up for God.
The Props: a picture of the Lone Ranger
Quick Summary: You'll use the story of Noah to encourage kids and adults to help each other stand up for God.

Ask everyone to stand up. Call out the following statements. When only one or two people are left standing, you can stop. If you reach the end of the list and several people are standing, call out specific information that will force them to sit down. For example, if Joe, Alberta, and Frank are all standing, you might say, "If your name is Joe or Alberta, sit down."

If you have blue eyes, sit down.

If you drove a red car to church today, sit down.

Sit down if you're wearing nail polish.

Sit down if you didn't bring your Bible.

If you love the (name your local football team), **sit down.**

Sit down if you ate cereal for breakfast.

Sit down if you have shoelaces on your shoes.

If you're wearing a wedding ring, sit down.

If you're chewing gum, sit down.

Ask the remaining person (or people):

   • **How does it feel to be the only one left standing?**

Say: **You can sit down with everyone else. Now turn to the people sitting nearby and tell about a time you felt like the only one. Maybe you were the only one who didn't have a date to prom when you were in high school, or you were the only one who had to stay in at recess.**

Allow about two minutes for people to share, then draw attention back to yourself.

Say: **There was a guy in the Bible who *really* felt like the odd man out.**

Let's check out Genesis 6:9. Encourage families to find Genesis 6:9 and read it together. Then ask:

- **How do you think Noah felt, being the *only one* who was righteous?**

- **Have you ever felt like Noah? In what way?**

Say: **Maybe you're the only Christian at your school. Maybe you're the only one in your office who goes to church. Maybe your family is the only one on the block who loves God. You may feel a bit like Noah...or this person.**

For Extra Impact

Project a picture of the Lone Ranger so the whole congregation can see it. Explain that the Lone Ranger was a pretend guy who fought crime in the Old West.

Hold up the picture of the Lone Ranger. Say: **The Lone Ranger was a superhero in the Wild West...but even *he* didn't have to go it alone. He had a helper named Tonto. And if you ever feel like Noah or the Lone Ranger Christian—just look around you.** (Pause.) **Look at all the Tontos who are here to stand with you.**

Stand up if you've ever prayed with someone.

Stand up if you've ever encouraged someone in his or her friendship with God.

Stand up if you're willing to help another Christian.

Stand up if you're willing to pray for Christians overseas.

Ask people to join hands with people near them so everyone is connected to someone else. Pray and thank God for the family of Christians that he's given to your church. Ask God to help your congregation members support and stand by each other.

Remind everyone to use the fun ideas in the Sticky Note bulletin inserts this week.

4. A Promise Reminder

The Passage: Genesis 9:1-17
The Point: We can trust in God's promises.
The Props: picture of a rainbow
Quick Summary: You'll use the story of the rainbow covenant to help families discover that God's promises last forever.

Say: **In just a moment I'd like you to find someone sitting nearby who's wearing a wedding ring. Let that person take about a minute or two to share a bit about how he or she got that ring. Ready? Go ahead.**

Allow up to two minutes for people to share their wedding ring stories, then draw attention to yourself.

Say: **I'll bet you heard some wonderful, romantic stories that showed how much two people loved each other. Those of you who shared, answer this question:**

• **When you look at your ring, what does it remind you of?**

Take a few responses and be sure to repeat them aloud so others can hear. Then continue: **A wedding ring is a reminder of someone's love, commitment, and the promise they made. Today let's explore another promise someone made.**

Hold up the picture of a rainbow. Ask:

• **When you see a rainbow, what does it remind you of?**

> ## For Extra Impact
> *Project a picture of a rainbow so the whole congregation can see it, rather than holding a picture.*

Say: **God actually created the rainbow to stand as a reminder of a promise. We can find more information in Genesis 9. God was so saddened by sin that he sent a flood that wiped out every living creature...except for Noah's family and the animals on the ark Noah had built. Imagine for a moment that you're part of Noah's family,** *after* **the flood.** Ask:

• **How do you think you'd feel every time you saw the sky get a little cloudy?**

Say: **God promised that he would never again destroy the earth with a flood. He told Noah and his family that whenever the clouds came, the** rainbow would also be in the sky as a reminder of his promise. Talk about this with someone sitting nearby. Ask:

• How does seeing a rainbow reminder of God's promise affect you?

After about a minute, draw attention to yourself.

Say: **The Bible is filled with incredible promises from God.** Ask members of the congregation to call out some of the promises God has made in Scripture. Be sure to repeat a few so that everyone can hear. Ask:

• How do these promises affect your relationship with God?

Say: **Just as a wedding ring is a reminder of someone's promise of love, your Bible can be a reminder of God's countless promises to us. This week, identify something that you see in everyday life—it might be a tree outside your house, the sunset, or even your children. Every time you see that, remember God's promise of love for you.**

Remind everyone to use the fun ideas in the Sticky Note bulletin inserts this week.

5. A Slice of Obedience

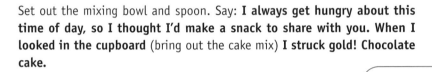

The Passage: Genesis 12:1-9

The Point: God has great plans for us, but we need to be willing to obey.

The Props: a box of chocolate cake mix, a bowl, a mixing spoon, a travel mug of coffee, Italian salad dressing, and an egg. Place the travel mug, salad dressing, and egg in a paper sack. For extra fun, you may also want to provide cupcakes for each person in the congregation.

Quick Summary: You'll use the story of Abram's call to help families explore ways that they may be resistant to God's plans.

Set out the mixing bowl and spoon. Say: **I always get hungry about this time of day, so I thought I'd make a snack to share with you. When I looked in the cupboard** (bring out the cake mix) **I struck gold! Chocolate cake.**

The box promises this delicious, mouth-watering cake. All I have to do is follow the instructions. Pour the cake mix into the bowl, then read the box. **First they tell me to add water to the cake mix.** Look around. **I don't have water, but this coffee should do just fine. After all, it's got water in it!** Dump the coffee into the bowl with the cake mix, then refer to the box again.

> ### For Extra Impact
> *Project a picture of a yummy-looking piece of chocolate cake.*

Now I'm supposed to put in some cooking oil. I don't really like cooking oil—it doesn't have a lot of flavor. Bring out the salad dressing. **This should work just as well. It's got oil in it,** *plus* **a whole lot of other seasonings and stuff.** Dump in a liberal amount of the oil. **And who needs to measure? I've got a pretty good eye for the measurements.**

Refer to the box again. **Finally, an egg. OK, now that one I've got.** Bring out the egg and add it—shell and all—to the bowl. **There, I've followed their directions. I can't** *wait* **to taste this cake!**

Talk about this with a few people sitting near you. Ask:

- **Why do you think my cake might taste different from the one pictured on the box?**

After about a minute, draw attention back to yourself and take a few responses from the congregation. Say: **The makers of the cake mix promised me something good—all I had to do was follow their directions. Hmmm. Sounds like something I read in the Bible.** Direct families to gather and read Genesis 12:1-3 together. Then ask:

- **What did God promise to Abram?**

- **What instructions did Abram have to follow?**

Say: **Abram packed up everything he owned and took a long journey across the desert. Was it inconvenient? Probably. Was it hard? Probably. Was it time-consuming? Yep. Was it worth it to receive God's blessing? Definitely!**

God had amazing blessings in store for Abram. Think for a minute about the blessings God has in store for *you*. Motion to the picture of the cake on the box. **Imagine that God's blessings are like this beautiful cake.** Motion to the mixing bowl. **Now think about the directions God is asking you to follow to receive his blessings.**

Maybe God is asking you to be friends with someone new at school.

Maybe God wants you to take a stand for your faith at the office.

Maybe God's directions are telling you to spend time in prayer. Ask:

- **Are you willing to obey God's directions to receive his blessings?**

Say: **When you leave today, think of the delicious life God has planned for you. Then commit to following God's directions for your life!**

If you choose, provide cupcakes as people exit the service.

Remind everyone to use the fun ideas in the Sticky Note bulletin inserts this week.

6. The Best of the Best

The Passage: Genesis 13

The Point: God is pleased when we give others our best.

The Props: 1 snack-sized candy bar for every 4 people,
                      baskets for holding the candy bars

Quick Summary: You'll use the story of Abram and Lot to help
                   families explore ways that they can give others
                   their best.

Say: **I brought a treat for us to enjoy this morning. Unfortunately, I don't think I have quite enough, so we'll have to do some sharing.** Gather with your family or a group of about four people. While kids and adults are forming groups of four, ask a few volunteers to help you give one snack-sized candy bar to each small group.

Say: **Have the youngest member of your group divide the candy bar as equally as possible among your group. Once you've got your piece of candy, go ahead and eat it.** Pause while group members divide and eat the candy. After about a minute, draw attention to yourself. Ask:

- **Do you feel like you got a fair and equal part of the candy? Why or why not?**

- **Who in your group got the biggest piece?**

Say: **Talk about this in your group. Why is it so hard for us to give someone else a better share of something?** Pause for a couple of minutes while families discuss the question. Then continue: **Today I want to share a Bible story with you about someone who gave away the best. In fact, he gave the best of the best!**

Open your Bible to Genesis 13. Explain that Abram was traveling to a land that God was going to give him. He had his entire family, *plus* his nephew Lot's family. Say: **Both of those families had herds and herds of animals. And animals need lots of food. And Abram and Lot realized that the land couldn't support all of those people and animals...**(hold up a bag of candy) **kind of like there wasn't enough food for each of us. So Abram and Lot decided to split up. And Abram let Lot choose which land he wanted. Wow! Let's see what Lot did.**

> ## Tip
> *Using candy for this activity* really *drives home the point and makes for a memorable experience. However, if you don't want to purchase candy for the congregation, you can simply distribute index cards and ask groups to imagine that the card is a candy bar.*

Read aloud Genesis 13:10-12. Ask:

- **Why did Lot choose the plain of Jordan?**

Say: **Let's see what Abram got.** Read aloud Genesis 13:14-17, then ask groups to discuss this question:

- **Who do you think got the better deal? Why?**

Say: **Abram was older and was kind of leading the trip. Surely he could have said, "Lot, I'll take this lush, green, beautiful valley over here." But he gave Lot first choice, and Lot took what looked to be the best. And Abram wasn't left high and dry. In fact, God gave him even more land *and* extra blessings!**

Think of times you can give someone else the best. Maybe it's deciding who gets the last—and biggest—slice of pizza. Or a better parking spot at the grocery store. Or a more lucrative account at work. Pause. **That's God's gift to you—the opportunity to bless someone else with the best. This week, plan to look for ways to bless someone else with the best. Then look for God's blessings to *you*!**

Remind everyone to use the fun ideas in the Sticky Note bulletin inserts this week.

7. More Than You Can Count

The Passage: Genesis 15
The Point: God knows what he's doing.
The Props: a picture of a very starry sky
Quick Summary: You'll use the story of the Lord's promise to Abram to guide families in discovering that they can trust God.

Say: **In the Bible, God made an incredible promise to a guy named Abram. In Genesis 15, God said to Abram, "Look up into the sky and count the stars if you can. That's how may descendants you will have!"**

Now we've got some people here who I'm sure are amazing counters. I want to show you something and see if you can count all the items. Don't miss any! Ready?

Show the picture of the starry sky for about 30 seconds. Then ask how many stars people were able to count.

For Extra Impact

Project a picture of a starry sky.

Say: **On a clear night, you can see about 3,000 stars just by using your eyes. Grab your basic telescope and that number jumps to about 100,000. That would've been pretty amazing for Abram—something he could really look forward to. Problem was...Abram didn't even have *one* descendant. No baby boy. No baby girl. And he and his wife were both getting older!** Show the picture of the stars again. Ask:

• **If you were Abram, what would you think of God's promise?**

• **Have *you* ever wondered if God *really* knew what he was doing?**

Say: **I'm sure Abram wondered if God was right. In the Bible, Abram asks God more than once, "How is this going to happen?" Night after night, Abram may have looked into that starry sky and wondered, "Really, God? Are you *really* going to give me that many descendants?"** Ask families to discuss this question:

• **What things are hardest for you to trust God with?**

Tip

If you want to go the extra mile, give each person a few star stickers to take with them. Encourage families to put these around the house as a reminder that God is in control.

After a couple of minutes, call time and take a few responses. Say: **Tonight, take your family outside and look up at the stars. As you gather there, pray about the areas where it's hard for you to trust God. Thank God for being in control and knowing what he's doing.**

Remind everyone to use the fun ideas in the Sticky Note bulletin inserts this week.

8. All for God

The Passage: Genesis 22:1-19
The Point: Give your best to God.
The Props: a laundry basket for holding valuable items
Quick Summary: You'll use the story of Abraham's willingness to sacrifice Isaac as you encourage families to give their best to God.

Say: **Gather with your family or with a few people sitting nearby. Look through your purses, wallets, and bags, and determine the most valuable thing your group has. It might be a watch you're wearing, a $50 bill in your wallet, or—if you're a kid—a prized baseball card you brought today.** Allow about a minute for groups to determine their most valuable possession.

> ## For Extra Impact
> *Project a picture of a pearl necklace or other valuable item.*

Say: **Now, I'd like the person in your group wearing the most red to bring the item forward and give it to me.** Hold out your basket and accept the items brought forward. When you've collected all the items, hand the basket to a trusted volunteer and have him or her take the basket out of sight. (Be sure your volunteer holds onto the basket until you call him or her back.) Ask:

- **How did you feel as you watched your most valuable possessions disappear?**

Say: **This reminds me of a story in the Bible.** Open your Bible to Genesis 22, and read aloud verses 1-2. Then say: **God asked for Abram's dearest, greatest treasure. Abram had prayed for and waited for Isaac...for countless years! Let's see what he did when God asked him to sacrifice Isaac. Read Genesis 22:3 aloud in your groups.** Pause while families read the passage. Ask:

- **What things did you notice in this passage?**

Say: **Abram got up early! He didn't drag his feet or ask God why. He even made sure he had enough wood for the sacrifice. Talk about this with your group, and be sure everyone has a chance to share.**

- **What do you think God is asking *you* to give him?**

- **Are you acting like Abram? Why or why not?**

After about three minutes, call time. Say: **Abram was willing to sacrifice—to give God—the thing he loved most. Let's find out what happened.**

Read aloud Genesis 22:9-13, then say: **When Abram showed that he was willing to give his best to God** (motion for your volunteer to enter the room), **God gave it right back. Have the person wearing the most red come back and retrieve your treasure.** Pause while everyone takes back the items.

Pray: **Loving God, you have blessed us with so much. Lord, loosen our grip on these things and show us how we can give them up to you. Help us to give you our very best, even when it's hard. In Jesus' name, amen.**

Remind everyone to use the fun ideas in the Sticky Note bulletin inserts this week.

9. Stand Firm

The Passage: Genesis 37:1-36

The Point: Stand up for what's right.

The Props: none

Quick Summary: You'll use the story of Joseph in the well to encourage families to stand up for what's right.

Say: **Find a partner, and decide which of you is taller.** Pause while participants pair up and determine which partner is taller. Continue: **Shorter partners, stand up. The taller partner will sit down, with his or her back against the back of the chair** [or pew], **feet flat on the ground, and arms crossed against his or her chest. Got it?** You may want to demonstrate the proper way to sit.

Say: **Now, if you're standing, press your index finger against your partner's forehead and push. When I say "go!" the person who's sitting will try to stand up without moving his or her feet. OK? Go!**

Most partners will be surprised to see how hard (or impossible) it is for the seated person to stand...even with just one finger holding them in place! After a few seconds, call time and ask a few partners:

• **What surprised you in this activity?**

Say: **Today we're talking about standing up for what's right. When we say "standing up," we aren't exactly talking about getting to your feet. Standing up for what's right means doing things God's way...even when no one else is. There's a guy in the Bible who had trouble standing up for what was right.**

Lead everyone in turning to Genesis 37:1-36. Say: **The Bible tells us about a guy named Jacob who had 12 sons. The oldest was Reuben. Second from the youngest was Joseph. Jacob loved Joseph the best. And to make it worse, Joseph had some incredible dreams in which he saw his brothers—or things representing his brothers—bowing down to him. That made them *really* annoyed at him! In fact, the Bible tells us that Joseph's brothers *hated* him!**

Joseph's brothers were watching the family sheep way out in the desert, and Joseph went to check on them. Let's see what happened

For Extra Impact

Project a picture of a well.

next. Read aloud Genesis 37:18-22. Ask people to discuss this question with those sitting nearby:

- **What do you think of the way Reuben stood up for Joseph?**

Say: **Think of the little index finger that held some of you in place.** Ask:

- **What held Reuben back from doing the right thing?**

Continue: **Well, Reuben's plan might have worked better if he'd stuck around! The brothers tossed Joseph in a well. Then Reuben went away, and while he was gone, the rest of the brothers decided to sell Joseph to a passing caravan. When Reuben came back to rescue his brother... he was gone!**

Reuben *did* keep Joseph alive, but by refusing to completely stand up to his brothers, he caused Jacob—their father—plenty of sorrow. *And* a lifetime separated from his son!

Hold up your index finger and ask each person to do the same.

Say: **Look at this little finger. It held someone in place in our experiment. Think about what little thing keeps *you* from standing up for what's right. What pushes you down when you know you should do things God's way?** Pause. **Link index fingers with the people sitting near you while I close in prayer.**

Pray: **Mighty Lord, sometimes we need your power to stand up for what's right. Small things can keep us from speaking up or acting in a way that's honoring to you. Please link us together and help us to strengthen each other. In Jesus' name, amen.**

Remind everyone to use the fun ideas in the Sticky Note bulletin inserts this week.

10. United

The Passage: Genesis 45:1-15

The Point: Forgiveness unites us.

The Props: two large posters, one with the word "Untied" written on it and the other with "United" written on it

Quick Summary: You'll use the story of Joseph forgiving his brothers to help families explore how forgiveness unites us.

Have children and adults form small groups of about six.

Say: **Find one person in your group who's wearing shoes with laces and send that person forward.** Pause while volunteers are sent forward.

Say: **Welcome to the** [name of your church] **first annual indoor race walk. Welcome, racers! I see that you're almost ready, wearing your best running shoes.** Show "racers" the course you want them to race—ideally just up one aisle and down another, or from one side of the church to the other. **Ready? On your mark, get set...wait! I almost forgot. First, I need you to untie your shoes.** Pause while racers unlace their shoes. When all the shoes are untied, direct racers to *carefully* walk the course you set out. **On your mark, get set, shuffle!**

When everyone has completed the race, lead those who are seated in a rousing round of applause for all of the racers. Send racers back to their groups, and have groups discuss the following questions:

- **What went through your mind when you knew this race would be with shoes untied?**

- **Why do runners keep *their* shoes tied?**

After a couple of minutes, call time and take a few responses from the audience. Then say: **When shoes are untied, things can get ugly. That's a lot like what happens when relationships get untied, too. There's a great example we can look at in the Bible.**

Open your Bible to Genesis 45 and explain that Jacob had 12 sons. Eleven of the sons got along pretty well, but they hated one of their brothers, Joseph. In fact, the brothers secretly sold Joseph into slavery and told their father that he'd died!

Say: **Joseph had plenty to be mad at his brothers about! Talk about a reason for unforgiveness. Yes, that family definitely was untied!**

Many, many years passed. Joseph actually worked his way up from slave, to prisoner, to the second in command of Egypt! God did incredible things through Joseph's life, including giving him wisdom to interpret dreams. Through this gift, Joseph helped Egypt survive a famine, when nearly no food would grow. Joseph's brothers came to Egypt to buy grain, since they couldn't grow any. Of course, they had no idea that Joseph was there...and in a place of incredible power. Ask:

• **If you were Joseph, what would you do?**

For Extra Impact

Project slides of the words "Untied" and "United."

Take a few responses, then continue: **Ultimately, Joseph forgave his brothers. And it wasn't just a quick "I forgive you." Joseph invited his brothers to live in Egypt where there was food. They got the best of the best land!** Show poster of the word "Untied." **You know, there's a funny thing about the word "untied." By making a small change, just switching the "i" and the "t,"** (pause while you switch to the poster of the word "United") **"untied" can become "united."** Pause. **Forgiveness does that. It unites our relationships. It ties up the loose, harmful things that cause us to stumble. It brings us back into relationship with others...and with God. This week, work at being united, not untied.**

Remind everyone to use the fun ideas in the Sticky Note bulletin inserts this week.

11. God Speaks

The Passage: Exodus 3

The Point: God speaks in many ways.

The Props: a cell phone

Quick Summary: You'll use the story of Moses and the burning bush to guide families in discovering ways that God speaks to us today.

Before this lesson, you may want to download a unique, familiar, or funny ringtone to your cell phone. You should also turn up the volume on the ringer as loud as possible. You'll need to arrange for someone to call you as soon as you get up to speak. The person should continue to call until you turn off the phone.

Stand up to speak, act annoyed or embarrassed when your cell phone rings, but just try to ignore it. After a while, turn the phone off.

Say: **Has that ever happened to you? You're just going about your job and the cell phone rings. Someone's just *got* to talk to you. Did you know that happened in the Bible? Well, it wasn't a cell phone exactly.**

You see, Moses was raised in the Pharaoh's palace but ran away and became a shepherd way out in the desert. He was calmly minding his own business, doing his job, when he saw a burning bush. But this wasn't just a brush fire. This bush didn't burn up! And when Moses got closer, *God* began speaking out of the fire!
Ask participants to discuss this question:

> ## For Extra Impact
> *Project a picture of a cell phone.*

• **Why do you think God chose to speak from a burning bush?**

Say: **The burning bush got Moses' attention** (hold up your phone) **kind of like the ringer on this cell phone got mine. Talk about this question:**

• **Do you think God still speaks to us today? How?**

Take a few responses from the audience, being sure to repeat them aloud so everyone can hear. Then say: **God *does* speak to us today...but it might be different for each person. Let me show you what I mean. If you've got a cell phone, take it out and get it ready to play your ringtone.** Pause. **In a minute, I want your family or the people near you to see how many different ringtones you can hear in 30 seconds. Ready? Go!**

After 30 seconds call time and have everyone put their cell phones back on "vibrate."

Say: **God may speak to you through his word, through a song, through the words of a brother or sister in Christ. God may speak to you in a sunset.** Play your ringtone and pause. **It doesn't matter** *how* **God speaks to you...but how you respond. Will you pick up and answer...**(turn off your phone) **or just turn away?**

This week, whenever you hear any phone ring, ask God to give you the courage to tune in and hear what he has to say.

Remind everyone to use the fun ideas in the Sticky Note bulletin inserts this week.

Sticky Faith

12. Powerful Plagues

The Passage: Exodus 7:14–10:29

The Point: God is powerful.

The Props: a picture of a muscleman

Quick Summary: You'll use the story of the first nine plagues to guide families in looking for modern-day signs of God's power.

Before this lesson, arrange for a volunteer (or team of volunteers) to turn out most of the lights in your meeting space. Set up a cue to use later in the lesson.

Say: **Today we're talking about power.** Show the picture of the muscleman. **You may think of *this* when you hear the word *power*. But I want to tell you about God's incredible, amazing, unparalleled power.**

For Extra Impact

Project a picture of a muscleman or a close-up of a bicep.

There was a time in the Bible when God told a man named Moses to lead the Israelites out of slavery. They'd been slaves to the Egyptians for about 400 years! But the king of Egypt was named Pharaoh, and he didn't like the idea of losing all those slaves they'd gotten used to having around. So God showed Pharaoh that he meant business!

First, God turned the water to blood. Gross! Show me what your face would look like if you turned on the faucet and blood came out. Pause and show off your best look of disgust.

I'm with you. Then God sent millions of frogs upon Egypt. If you're wearing green, jump up and down at least one time and say, "ribbit." Pause.

But God was just beginning to flex his muscles. Next God sent annoying gnats—let's have all the men and boys buzz. Pause. **Keep buzzing because God wasn't done yet! God sent zillions of flies, too. Ladies and girls, now let's hear you buzz.** After a few seconds of buzzing, direct everyone to stop.

But Pharaoh thought *he* had the power...big mistake. Each time God sent one of these plagues—or bad things—to the Egyptians, Pharaoh told Moses, "No, the Israelites can't leave."

God sent a disease that killed all of the Egyptian's cattle. How about a nice "moo" in remembrance of the cattle? Lead everyone in saying, "Mooo."

Then the Egyptians *themselves* **got sick with disgusting boils all over their skin. God sent hail that pounded the life out of the Egyptians' crops. Slap your legs to make the sound of hail.** Pause, then direct everyone to stop. **And any bits of grain left over after the hail...well, those got eaten by the swarms of locusts that God sent next.**

Finally, God plunged the land of Egypt into darkness. Motion for your assistant to turn out the lights. Pause in the darkness. **God's power was amazing. And shocking to the Egyptians. It showed Pharaoh who** *really* **was in control. Isn't it good to know that God is in control?**

In the darkness, think about how you've seen God's power in your life. Turn to someone nearby and whisper ways you see God's power. Think of as many examples as you can in one minute. After one minute, call time and have your volunteer turn the lights on.

God's power can be beautiful, scary, sweet, colorful, and breathtaking. We serve a powerful God. Let's worship God and praise him for his incredible power that's still evident in our world today.

Lead everyone in singing a worship song about God's power, such as "Awesome God" or "A Mighty Fortress Is our God." Then remind them to use the fun ideas in the Sticky Note bulletin inserts this week.

13. Passover Protection

The Passage: Exodus 12

The Point: God protects us.

The Props: Depending on the size of your meeting space, you'll need several spray bottles. You'll also need water to fill the sprayers.

Quick Summary: You'll use the story of the first Passover to demonstrate how God protects us today by sending Jesus to take away our sins.

Round up a few volunteers to help you. Give each one a spray bottle filled with water, and station your sprayers at the front of the sanctuary.

Say: **Today I want to share an incredible—and true—Bible story with you. It happened when God's people the Israelites were slaves in Egypt. God chose Moses to lead the people out of Pharaoh's control. But Pharaoh had been stubborn and wouldn't let the people go. God sent one final, horrible punishment upon Egypt.**

God told the Israelites to gather with their families. Do that now. Gather with *your* **family, or with a few people sitting near you.** Pause. **God's people were to sacrifice a perfect lamb and spread its blood over their doorposts. They were to eat the lamb and some other special foods. Then they were to get ready to leave. That night, God would send his angel of death throughout the land. The homes marked with the lamb's blood would be spared. Homes that didn't bear the mark—well, something else waited for them. The firstborn male in that household would die.** Pause.

In a minute, my team of sprayers is going to send water to "pass over" you. I want the biggest person in your group to stand in a way that will protect the rest of you from the water. Pause while people move. **Ready?** Allow the sprayers to spray over the group, not aiming at individuals but spraying *over* everyone so the water falls down. After 30 seconds, have the sprayers stop. Have groups talk about these questions together:

- **What were you thinking as you huddled together for protection?**

Tip

It's important to choose a water sprayer that doesn't resemble a gun.

For Extra Impact

Project a picture of a Super Soaker or spray bottle.

- How did it feel to try to protect your family or group?

- How was this like or unlike what the Israelites must have felt?

Say: I imagine that it was pretty scary in those Israelite homes. Even though they trusted God, this was a test they *didn't* want to fail. But God protected them—better than some of you could protect your groups in this experience! Ask:

- What does God's protection look like today?

Say: Even though bad things still happen, God does protect us today. Just as the Israelites sacrificed a perfect lamb to provide the blood that bought their protection...God sacrificed his perfect Son, Jesus. The blood of Jesus covers and protects us...perfectly. When we choose to believe in Jesus and ask for his forgiveness, it's as if his blood is marked on the doorposts of our hearts. We're protected—we're spared—from an eternity away from God.

Tip

This is a great time to present the message of salvation, using your church's language or traditions.

God wants us to cling to him, to huddle under his protection. When we claim Jesus as our perfect Passover lamb, we can enjoy God's perfect protection.

Remind everyone to use the fun ideas in the Sticky Note bulletin inserts this week.

Sticky Faith

14. Just Stand Still

The Passage:	Exodus 14:15-31
The Point:	Wait on the Lord.
The Props:	a picture of the modern-day Red Sea, a towel, several ice chests filled with ice, a thawed Otter Pop, a frozen Otter Pop for each member of the congregation, towels (you'll get your clothes dirty, so you may want to wear older clothes), and a handful of volunteers to help you distribute the Otter Pops
Quick Summary:	You'll use the story of the Red Sea escape to help families discover what it means to wait on God... and why it's sometimes hard for us to do that.

Say: **Today we're going to look at the Bible book of Exodus. The word "exodus" means "exit" or "departure," and that's what this book is all about! The Israelites, God's chosen people, had been slaves in Egypt for about 400 years. After God showed his power, the king—Pharaoh—finally let the people go free. The book of Exodus is about their...exit!**

God used a man named Moses to guide and lead the Israelites. First they went into the desert, but then they ran into something that blocked their exit. Show the picture of the Red Sea.

Bible scholars aren't exactly sure which sea the Israelites needed to cross, but the Bible is pretty clear that it was a huge body of water, too big for two million people to get across very easily. To make matters worse, Pharaoh suddenly missed all those slaves who used to work for him—and sent a pretty tough army after them. The Israelites were trapped! And they were none too happy about it.

Call out what you would say if *you* were one of the Israelites.

After hearing a few responses, say: **You sound a lot like the Israelites. They cried out for help, complaining that they were better off as slaves! Listen to what Moses told the people.** Read aloud Exodus 14:13a: **"But Moses told the people, 'Don't be**

> **Tip**
> *You may want to have a few volunteers cut the tops off of the frozen Otter Pops so the snack is easier for folks to eat right away.*

> **Tip**
> *If you're doing this lesson in the winter and can't find Otter Pops (or it's too cold for a frozen snack), use brownies. Talk about how you didn't want to wait for the batch to cook, then show a blob of semi-baked dough. Gross!*

afraid. Just stand still and watch the Lord rescue you today.' " Pause. Just stand still. Turn to a few people sitting near you and talk about this question.

For Extra Impact

Project a picture of the Red Sea or another wide expanse of water.

• **When is it hard for you to just stand still and wait?**

Allow about three minutes for discussion, then call time and take a few responses. Then continue: **Sometimes we want things right away. I've brought one of my favorite treats today.** Bring out the thawed Otter Pop. **Some of you might like these, too. They're icy and refreshing and sweet... mmmmm! The only down side is that they don't come frozen. You have to wait for them. But me...I didn't feel like waiting this morning. So I'm going to enjoy mine right away.** Cut off the top of the plastic and squeeze the Otter Pop so the juice squirts all over you. Ask:

• **What happened?**

• **Why didn't I get to enjoy my nice, icy, refreshing treat?**

Say: **While I clean up here, go ahead and talk about this with the people sitting nearby.** Ask:

• **Why does God sometimes need us to wait for *his* timing?**

While people are talking, try to clean up as much as possible with the towel. After a minute or so, call time and hold up the frozen Otter Pop.

Say: **This Otter Pop sat in my freezer all night. For like 12 hours. That's a *long* time to wait for a refreshing snack. I sure hope it's worth it.**

Cut the top off of the plastic, and squeeze up the frozen Otter Pop. Take a satisfied bite. Say: **Yep—it's perfect! I don't want to enjoy this all by myself.** Motion to your volunteers to hand out the frozen Otter Pops as quickly as possible. When everyone has one, say: **While you have a nice, icy, refreshing treat, I want to tell you what happened when the Israelites waited on God.** Read aloud Exodus 14:21-31 from a kid-friendly Bible translation.

God's timing isn't our timing. He has incredible plans for us—but sometimes we have to wait. Take a bite of your Otter Pop. **But God's timing is always worth the wait.**

Remind everyone to use the fun ideas in the Sticky Note bulletin inserts this week.

15. Just Enough

The Passage: Exodus 16:11-21

The Point: God provides what we need.

The Props: Frosted Flakes (about ¼ cup per person), resealable plastic baggies, a ¼ cup measuring cup

Quick Summary: You'll use the story of God providing quail and manna to show families that God is faithful to provide what we need.

Before people arrive, have a team of helpers assist you in scooping about ¼ cup of Frosted Flakes cereal into resealable plastic baggies. Seal the bags, and then scatter them around the sanctuary. Plan to have assistants on hand with extra bags.

Say: **The Israelites were God's chosen people. He'd led them out of slavery, provided an amazing escape from the Egyptians, and taken them into the safety of the desert. Here, God began to teach the people *his* incredible plan for them. But the people had other...issues. Let's read about them together.** Direct families to open their Bibles to Exodus 16:2-3. Read the passage aloud while families follow along.

Continue: **Sometimes we're kind of hard on the Israelites. We think they should have had such a fantastic faith when *we* are just as whiny! But God is good—let's see how God responded.** Lead families in reading Exodus 16:13-14.

Say: **I thought this passage might make you hungry, so I've provided a tasty morsel for you, too. Find a few people sitting near you, and form a group. Then choose the person in your group who ate the biggest breakfast.** Pause. **Send this person out to find "manna" for each of you. Just enough for each person!**

For Extra Impact

Project a picture of a box of cereal.

Pause while the "big breakfast eaters" search for and retrieve the "manna." Everyone can eat his or her snack while discussing the following questions:

- **Why did God provide food for the Israelites?**

- **What do you think the Israelites *expected* God to provide?**

After a couple of minutes, draw attention back to yourself. Say: **God provided just what the Israelites needed—bread and meat. He told them to take what they needed for each day and not to try to store up more.** Ask:

- **Why do you think God provided just enough for each day?**

Take a few responses, then continue: **Suppose this "manna" I've given you had all the nutrients your body needed. Imagine what it would be like to eat it for the next 40 years.** Pause.

Sometimes we expect God to fulfill our every wish, like a genie in a bottle. God has promised to give us what we *need*. **We're like the Israelites, too—storing up more than we need so we won't have to rely on God for that next day's portion. Silently consider this:**

- **How would your faith grow if you depended on God to provide what you need each day?**

Close in prayer, asking God to give us the faith to know that he'll provide all that we need.

Remind everyone to use the fun ideas in the Sticky Note bulletin inserts this week.

16. Stay Inside the Lines

The Passage: Exodus 20:1-17

The Point: The Ten Commandments give us good guidelines for following God.

The Props: photocopies of a coloring page featuring a horse, crayons (a handful for each family), blank paper, resealable plastic bags

Quick Summary: You'll use the story of the Ten Commandments to help families discover that God's rules give us good guidelines for living a life that pleases him.

Before people arrive, make photocopies of the picture of the horse. You'll need one page per person. Place a handful of crayons into resealable plastic bags, and set out the bags and sheets of blank paper on the chairs or pews.

Say: **Today we're going to start with a little art. I want each of you to draw a beautiful, colorful picture of a horse. You'll find the supplies you need on the chairs** [or pews]. Pause while people find the materials. **You've got one minute...go!** After a minute, call time and have people share their drawings with the people sitting nearby. Ask:

> ### For Extra Impact
> *Project a picture of a horse.*

• **What was challenging about this?**

Say: **Sounds like we need to try this a different way.** Ask several volunteers to help you hand out the coloring picture of the horse. Continue: **Now I'll give you a minute to give me a beautiful, colorful picture of a horse. Go ahead.** After a minute, call time and ask:

• **How was this experience different from drawing your own horse?**

Take a few responses, then say: **In the Bible, God painted a picture of a good way to live for his chosen people. We call that passage the Ten Commandments. Sometimes we think of the Ten Commandments as restrictions or hard-to-follow rules. But think of this coloring page.** Hold up a sample of the horse coloring page. **I gave you guidelines to fill in. I gave you a shape to follow. The end result was a beautiful picture... especially if you stayed inside the lines!**

God's Ten Commandments are just that—lines or boundaries to guide us in a healthy life that will please God. Read aloud Exodus 20:1-17 from a kid-friendly Bible translation. Ask families to talk about this question:

- **How will my life be better by following the Ten Commandments?**

Close in prayer, thanking God for giving the Ten Commandments to guide our lives and keep us closer to him.

Remind everyone to use the fun ideas in the Sticky Note bulletin inserts this week.

17. Grab Hold

The Passage: Numbers 13:25–14:9
The Point: Trust God.
The Props: about 20 tennis balls
Quick Summary: You'll use the story of the spies in the Promised Land to help families realize that we need to reach out and act in faith.

Say: **Let's play a game today. I've got a bucket of tennis balls that I'm going to throw to you.** Call on about 20 people to stand up (this prevents people from diving over each other to get one of the balls). **I'll do my best to get them into your hands, OK?**

Toss the tennis balls one at a time to each of your "catchers." When everyone has caught (or attempted to catch) a ball, applaud your volunteers. Say: **Now, it's your turn! If you caught the ball, it's your turn to throw it back to me, nice and gently. Ready?** When your volunteers throw the balls, *do not* reach out to catch them. (You may need to sidestep a ball if it's thrown very hard, but try not to move.) When all the balls have been thrown, let your volunteers sit down.

Say: **I can't believe that I didn't catch any of those tennis balls! I thought you guys were going to throw them to me!** Pause, then ask:

• **What's wrong with my attitude?**

Say: **I want to pause here and take you to a story in the Bible. It's in Numbers, when the Israelites were getting ready to take the Promised Land. We call it the Promised Land because God had promised it to the Israelites long ago.**

Moses sent 12 spies to check out the land. They looked at the people living in the land, the food there, and the landscape. Then they brought back their report. The land was awesome—flowing with milk and honey, pomegranates, figs, and grapes. But the people...they're huge! We can't take this land. No way. In fact, here's what the people said. Read aloud Numbers 14:3-4. Ask:

• **What was wrong with the Israelites' attitude?**

Pick up a tennis ball and say: **In our game, when I threw the ball, each person catching reached out to grab the ball. But when it was my turn to catch, I just stood here. Talk about this with your neighbors:**

• **How did I remind you of the Israelites in this passage?**

After a minute, draw attention back to yourself.

Say: **Trusting God is an action. We have to reach out and take hold of God's promises. How foolish it is for me to stand here and let you toss something to me...and I let it fall by the wayside. Or worse, smack me in the face. God has thrown us some pretty amazing truths. Call out some of the things God has promised to us.** Repeat the responses you hear so others can hear them. Then ask:

• **How are you going to show that you believe those truths?**

Pray: **Loving God, thank you for all the things you've promised to us. Lord, give us the strength, wisdom, and courage to believe those things and to live with a trusting attitude. In Jesus' name, amen.**

Remind everyone to use the fun ideas in the Sticky Note bulletin inserts this week.

18. 100 Percent

The Passage: Deuteronomy 6:5-6

The Point: Give God 100 percent of yourself.

The Props: a toy car

Quick Summary: You'll use God's command to the Israelites to show families what it means to give God all we are.

Say: **I'm really excited today because I've got a new car. Yep, brand new, shiny, sporty, and very cool. I'm so excited that I'm going to give each and every one of you a ride in it! Just wait 'til you see my car!**

Hold up the toy car. Ask:

- **Where do you think we can go in my new car?**

Say: **You don't seem as excited as you were before. What's up?** Take a few responses. **My car is real. Check out those cars in the parking lot—they've got doors and tires and windows...just like mine!** Ask:

- **What's the difference between the cars in the parking lot and my car?**

Say: **I think you're catching on!** Hold up the car. **This car looks like a car, but it's not a 100 percent real, authentic car. God had something to say about being 100 percent, too.** Lead families in opening their Bibles to Deuteronomy 6:5-6, and ask families to read the passage together. Then ask:

- **What was God asking of his people? Why?**

Say: **God commanded his people to love him 100 percent. He didn't want devotion that was small, halfhearted, or given with a shrug. He wanted the real deal.** Hold up the toy car. **No toy car devotion would do!** Ask families to discuss these questions:

- **What kind of devotion does God expect from you today?**

- **What percentage have you given God?**

Say: **My car, it looks pretty good. Sometimes our devotion to God can *look* good. But this car, on the inside it's just plastic pictures of an engine. Think about this silently:**

> ## For Extra Impact
>
> *Project a picture of a Matchbox car that looks pretty real but is recognizable as a toy.*

- **If God were to look deeper, into your heart, what would he see?**

Pause, then say: **Today I'm challenging you to live out this passage. In the New Testament, Jesus called this the most important piece of Scripture. Let's say this Scripture together and commit to giving God 100 percent.**

Lead everyone in standing and saying Deuteronomy 6:5-6 together a few times.

Remind everyone to use the fun ideas in the Sticky Note bulletin inserts this week.

19. Stuck To You!

The Passage: Joshua 1:1-9

The Point: God is always with us.

The Props: about five dot stickers per person

Quick Summary: You'll use the story of the Lord's charge to Joshua to remind families that God is always with us.

Direct families to open their Bibles to Joshua 1:1-9. Say: **This is an awesome part of Scripture because it's so reassuring to us today. The Israelites had been wandering in the desert for 40 years, waiting to enter the land God had promised them. They could have entered it 40 years before, but they hadn't trusted God. Now Moses had died and Joshua was getting ready to lead the nation into the land...and into the future. Call out some words that might describe how Joshua felt.**

For Extra Impact

Project a picture of a vast desert.

Let people call out words. Repeat them so everyone can hear, then continue: **I think Joshua probably *did* feel** [some of the words called out]. **But God had it covered. Let's read this together. Every time you hear something that would be encouraging to Joshua, I want you to give someone a high five. Ready?** Read Joshua 1:5-9 aloud, pausing for people to give high fives. Ask:

- **What did God promise Joshua?**

- **If you were Joshua, how would you have felt after hearing this straight from the mouth of God?**

Say: **This passage is true for us today. God sticks with us—he never leaves us. He wants us to be strong and do the things he's set before us. I want you to remember that God sticks with us. So we're going to get a little wild this morning. I need someone from each family or group of five people to come up and get a sheet of stickers for each person in your family or group.**

After you've distributed stickers, continue: **When I say "go," you'll have 10 seconds to stick your stickers to the people in your family or group. Ready? Go!**

After 10 seconds, call time and direct everyone to stop sticking stickers to others. Say: **Look around. You all look crazy! There are stickers everywhere!** Ask:

- **What's going to happen to these stickers?**

- **How is that different from the way God sticks with us?**

Say: **Keep your stickers on you as long as you can. You know, these stickers will fall off—but they can still remind us of God. Every time a sticker falls off, remember that God is still with you.**

Read aloud Joshua 1:9 again.

Remind everyone to use the fun ideas in the Sticky Note bulletin inserts this week.

20. March!

The Passage: Joshua 6:1-20

The Point: Obey God.

The Props: a picture of the city of Jericho (or another ancient-looking city)

Quick Summary: You'll use the story of the Israelites conquering Jericho to teach families the importance of obeying God even when we're weary of doing good.

Say: **Most of you are familiar with the story of Joshua leading the Israelites around Jericho. Jericho was one of the first cities in the Promised Land that God would give to the Israelites.** Show the picture of Jericho. **The city of Jericho covered about nine acres—that's about seven football fields! Imagine that you're all the Israelites—or at least a handful of them. You wake your kids up early in the morning, strap on your sandals, and head out for a *long* walk. Stand up and let's walk.**

Lead everyone in standing and marching in place. People should continue to march while you talk.

Say: **Back in Bible times, people would circle a city as part of laying siege to the city. That way, no one could get in or out of the city. But for the entire nation of Israel to march around the city...that was kind of different. But Joshua and the Israelites obeyed. Keep those knees up as you march! We've still got a ways to go.** Pause. **Sun feeling hot yet? Anyone tired yet? Are any kids asking, "Are we there yet?"** Pause. **OK, maybe you've made it around for one day. Have a seat.**

The Israelites marched around the city one time each day for six days. Then on the seventh day, they marched around the city *seven* times! Get up and march again. Pause and lead families in marching in place again. Remind them to keep their knees high and move quickly. **Oh, but God said to do it *silently*! How many of you think you could stay completely silent and not say a single word for that long?** Pause. **On the other days, we marched around seven football fields. Today, since we're marching seven times, it's like marching around a whole bunch *more* football fields!** Pause. **How are those feet going to feel when you've finished? Since you're not *really* the Israelites, I'm going to let you talk while you march. Talk with someone nearby about this:**

For Extra Impact

Project a picture of a blazing sun.

• **What do you think the Israelites were thinking as they marched?**

Allow about 30 seconds for discussion, and continue to remind everyone to keep marching while they talk.

Then say: **OK, you can sit down. This reminds me of Galatians 6:9a.** Read aloud Galatians 6:9a: **"So let's not get tired of doing what is good."** I'll bet the Israelites got tired of doing what God had told them to do. Think about this silently. Ask:

• **When do you get tired of obeying God?**

• **What keeps you "marching"?**

Say: **The Israelites saw a huge city filled with people who actually had a home; the Israelites had been nomads for 40 years! And God's instructions didn't seem too exciting or warlike—they might have just felt tiring. But when the Israelites obeyed, God handed the city of Jericho over to them.**

Sometimes we feel like there are big obstacles in our way...and God's way doesn't seem very logical. Today I want to encourage all you weary marchers to keep going. Keep obeying God even when you're weary. Let's close by saying Galatians 6:9a together. Turn to someone nearby and say this Scripture as an encouragement to him or her:

"So let's not get tired of doing what is good!"

Remind everyone to use the fun ideas in the Sticky Note bulletin inserts this week.

21. Wimpy Weapons

The Passage: Judges 7:1-22

The Point: God accomplishes his purpose in our lives.

The Props: deflated balloons, one for each person

Quick Summary: You'll use this story of Gideon's army facing the Midianites to help church members experience what it might have been like to be part of the victory God gave Gideon's army.

Have volunteers give each person a deflated balloon as he or she walks in.

Have families blow up and tie off their balloons. Explain how God equipped Gideon's army with the most unlikely and seemingly unhelpful weapons imaginable—trumpets, clay pots, and torches. Say: **Fighting a vast army of armored soldiers with pots and torches would be much like trying to wage a war with balloons. Let me show you how ridiculous that would feel.**

Direct families to "attack" the families around them by throwing their balloons at each other. After a few minutes of laughter and mayhem, have each person hold a balloon.

As you hold a pin near a balloon, say: **We just proved that there's very little harm that comes from a balloon. But there are some of you who feel real fear or at least a little bit of apprehension that I might pop this balloon. If I asked you to pop your balloon with your bare hands, some of you might feel afraid, too. I don't think you could win a war with a balloon, but if you use it just right, you can cause fear.**

With God's power and strategy, pots, torches, and horns became some of the most devastating weapons ever imagined. God has the creativity, knowledge, and power to use whatever he has given us to accomplish his purpose for our lives.

Remind everyone to use the fun ideas in the Sticky Note bulletin inserts this week.

For Extra Impact

Project an image of a shofar-like trumpet, a clay pot, and a torch.

22. Stuck On You

The Passage: Ruth 1:1-18

The Point: Families need to stick together.

The Props: none

Quick Summary: Families will discover that they need to choose to stick together even when it's difficult.

Instruct everyone to sit with their families and close friends. Say: **There are two big differences between your friends and your family members. First, you can't always choose your family members. Second, your family will be your family for the rest of your life. In the book of Ruth, Ruth realized the importance of family. She made the choice to stick with Naomi, her mother-in-law, even in a difficult situation.**

Read aloud Ruth 1:16-17. Then say: **Like Ruth and Naomi, your family is going to face various challenges. To make it through, you're going to need to stick together. Let me show you what I mean.**

Give family members the following challenge: **Find one person in your family or church family. Stand back to back and link arms. Then see how quickly you can go to the opposite side of the room then go back to your seat without knocking each other or anyone else over.**

When most people have returned to their seats, have families or groups of three or four discuss:

- **What difficulties are we facing right now that we need to help each other through? How can we stick together through this?**

- **How can the family best stick by you right now?**

Allow time for each person to respond. Then pray for God to strengthen the bonds of family in your church.

Remind everyone to use the fun ideas in the Sticky Note bulletin inserts this week.

23. Matters of the Heart

The Passage: 1 Samuel 16:1-13
The Point: God looks at the heart.
The Props: none
Quick Summary: Church members will take a look at what's in their
                     hearts and learn that that is what matters most to
                     God.

Summarize 1 Samuel 16:1-13, then read 1 Samuel 16:7 aloud.

Say: **Have each person in your family or a friend sitting near you show the inside of something he or she has. You can show what you have inside your wallet, purse, pocket, or even the inside of your shoe.** Pause.

Now, with your family or group, discuss the following:

> ## For Extra Impact
> *Project a picture of a large heart shape.*

- **Pick one of the things you found, and discuss how that item could represent something inside your heart that you wish wasn't there. For example, a short piece of string in someone's pocket could symbolize a short temper.**

- **Pick another item you found, and discuss how that item could represent something inside your heart that you're glad about. For example, a donor heart on your driver's license could stand for the deep love you have for each family member.**

Give people time to discuss. Then say: **God sees everything in your heart, and he loves you just the same. Let's take a moment to ask God to change the things we want changed and to thank him for the things inside our hearts we're glad about.**

Remind everyone to use the fun ideas in the Sticky Note bulletin inserts this week.

24. Facing the Giants

The Passage: 1 Samuel 17:1-50

The Point: God gives us the power to overcome our fears.

The Props: a few sheets of paper for each person

Quick Summary: Church members will write down their fears and pretend to throw them at "Goliath" as a way of declaring the victory they have through God's power.

As families enter your church, give each person a few sheets of paper. Summarize David's situation as he faced Goliath, as found in 1 Samuel 17:1-50.

Say: **While David showed tremendous courage and faith, he probably had moments of fear as he stood before the giant. Some of you are facing a giant right now in your lives—a fear that things may work out a certain way or that something might happen that you dread. Write or draw a picture of a fear you have on a sheet of paper we've given you. Then write another fear on another sheet. You can write as many fears as you like. If you run out of paper, just add more fears to each sheet.**

Have family members or friends each choose one fear to share with the others around them. After everyone has shared, encourage families and friends to take a moment to pray for one another.

For Extra Impact

Project a picture of Goliath on your screen for people to throw their paper fears at.

Read 1 Samuel 17:45. Say: **You aren't facing this fear alone. You are facing it in the name of the Lord. Crumple up that fear right now. When I count to 3, pretend to throw it at a giant up here with all your might. 1...2...3!**

Tell church members that the fear no longer belongs to them, but that they are now moving forward in the strength of the Lord and can overcome that fear by his power.

Remind everyone to use the fun ideas in the Sticky Note bulletin inserts this week.

25. Extend the Olive Branch

The Passage: 1 Samuel 25:2-35
The Point: God wants us to live in peace with each other.
The Props: a small stick for each person and rubber band for each family
Quick Summary: Church members will seek forgiveness and make peace with each other and family members.

Before your teaching, purchase a few wreaths made from vines or sticks from a hobby store. Cut the wreaths into 4- to 6-inch pieces. As families arrive, give each person a stick and each family a rubber band.

Summarize the account of Abigail making peace for Nabal as found in 1 Samuel 25:2-35.

Say: **When we say we are going to "extend the olive branch," we mean that we are going to make an offer for peace. It is possible that the olive branch has come to symbolize peace because the olive tree lives a very long time and outlasts wars. Today is a chance for you to extend the olive branch to members of your family.**

Encourage each person to give the stick to someone he or she has offended or sinned against. Encourage your church members to ask for forgiveness for the specific event as they extend their branches. Church members who don't know the people around them can share in generalities about a situation in which they need to forgive someone.

After everyone has shared, encourage each family or group to use the rubber band to bind the branches into the shape of a cross. Explain how we now have peace with God through the sacrifice Jesus made for us on the cross.

Remind everyone to use the fun ideas in the Sticky Note bulletin inserts this week.

26. I Declare a Thumb War

The Passage: 1 Kings 18

The Point: God is more powerful than anything.

The Props: none

Quick Summary: Families will play a fun game together as they discover how powerful God is.

> ## For Extra Impact
>
> *Project a picture of a thumb.*

Say: **We're going to have a contest to see who is the most powerful person in each family or area. With your family or the people around you, have a quick Thumb War tournament. You can thumb wrestle each person in the group around you once, and the person who wins the most matches is the most powerful person. If you're unable to engage in a Thumb War, you can choose to have a Rock, Paper, Scissors contest instead.**

If you have time and your church is really enjoying the contest, you can have the winners wrestle each other to find the most powerful person in your church. Say: **It appears that we have some world-class thumb wrestlers here. I think we've found some really powerful people. There was another contest that happened thousands of years ago that clearly showed who had the real power. It was much more final, impressive, and clear than a Thumb War—there was no question at the end of this contest who had the real power.**

Summarize the contest between Elijah and the prophets of Baal as found in 1 Kings 18.

Say: **God's display of power was so much greater than any display we can muster—including the display of the strongest thumb. God showed that there is no power in creation that matches his power. And God still shows us his power today.** Have families discuss:

- **How have you seen God's matchless power demonstrated today?**

- **How have you seen God's power in your life?**

Remind everyone to use the fun ideas in the Sticky Note bulletin inserts this week.

27. Do What?

The Passage: 2 Kings 5:1-19

The Point: We need to follow God's instructions even when we don't understand.

The Props: none

Quick Summary: Families will give each other silly challenges that remind them of how Naaman felt when Elisha told him to wash in the Jordan River seven times.

Have church members gather in families or form groups of about four or five.

Say: **We're going to play a game of Silly Add-On. The oldest person in your group must make a challenge that the next oldest person must complete. For example, you could twist your tongue into a "U," cross your eyes, or make a sound using your armpit and hand. The second oldest person must do his or her best to complete the silly challenge then add-on another challenge. The third oldest person must complete both challenges and add-on another challenge. The silly add-ons should just keep going until everyone has added on two challenges.**

Give groups a few minutes to play the game.

Say: **There was a great soldier and leader who once was given instructions that seemed just as silly as the instructions you just gave each other. Naaman had traveled from the land of Aram to Samaria because he heard that the prophet Elisha could help heal him of leprosy.**

Naaman was a bigwig in his country of Aram. He was used to royal treatment and expected the same from the prophet of Israel. But Elisha didn't even come outside to meet Naaman. Let's look at what Elisha did.

Read 2 Kings 5:9-12. Then have families discuss:

- **Why do you think Naaman refused to follow Elisha's instructions?**

- **Have you ever been asked to do something that didn't make sense to you? What happened?**

- **Why do you think Elisha gave these silly-sounding instructions to Naaman?**

For Extra Impact

Project a picture of a muddy river.

Say: **Fortunately, Naaman's servants convinced him to follow Elisha's directions. After Naaman obeyed, his leprosy was completely healed. Naaman learned that it's essential to follow God's commands—even when we don't completely understand them.**

Remind everyone to use the fun ideas in the Sticky Note bulletin inserts this week.

28. Who Are You?

The Passage: Nehemiah 9:17b

The Point: Take a closer look at who God is and who we are.

The Props: an index card and pencil for each person

Quick Summary: Church members will look at their identities and then at how God describes himself.

Have volunteers distribute a card to each person as he or she arrives. Say: **Let's take a minute to describe ourselves. On your card, write three things that describe who you are. You might list your occupation, your hobbies, and your favorite food.**

Give everyone a minute or two to write. Then have people form groups of about 10. Have one person in each group collect the cards, mix them up, and redistribute them. Challenge group members to try to guess the person described on each card. (Adults may need to help children.) Allow a few minutes.

Say: **The information on your cards provides a little glimpse into who you are. You've listed some of the things that make you...you. But there's a lot more to you and your family than the items you listed on the cards. With your family or with two or three others seated around you, discuss the following questions:**

- **If you had to describe who you are in just a few sentences, what would you say?**

- **How would you describe who your family is in just a few sentences?**

Say: **In Nehemiah 9:17b, God gives us a description of his character. He gives us a short picture of what makes God...God. He says that he is "a God of forgiveness, gracious and merciful, slow to become angry, and rich in unfailing love."**

With your family or group, discuss:

- **If you were going to describe God in a few sentences, what would you say?**

- **How does that description compare to what God says about himself in Nehemiah 9:17b?**

Remind everyone to use the fun ideas in the Sticky Note bulletin inserts this week.

29. Timing Is Everything

The Passage:	Esther 4
The Point:	God has a plan for you.
The Props:	blue, white, and yellow paper (available at office supply stores)
Quick Summary:	Your audience will help you tell Esther's story by providing sound effects.

As people enter, have volunteers randomly give each person a colored piece of paper. Hold a copy of each sheet as you speak.

Say: **You'll use your sheet of paper to help me tell the story of Esther, a beautiful Jewish wife of King Xerxes. Esther heard that Xerxes—who didn't know she was Jewish—planned to kill the Jews in her country. So she risked her life by begging Xerxes to spare her people. Esther wasn't sure about taking the risk until her Uncle Mordecai asked, "What if God made you queen for just this reason?"**

God had a special plan for Esther!

If you have a white sheet of paper, make the sound of wind by softly rubbing the sheet between your hands like this. Let's practice. Pause and practice.

If you have blue paper, snap your paper like this to make the sound of banners snapping in the wind. Let's practice. Pause and practice.

If you have yellow paper, make the sound of knocking at a door by flicking your paper like this. Let's practice. Pause and practice.

Make your sound when I hold up a sheet of paper that's the same color as yours. Stop making the noise when I lower the paper.

For Extra Impact

Project a picture of an Arabic or ancient-looking door.

Read the following aloud:

Esther knew that if she interrupted the king, she might be killed.

She walked out of her room (hold up WHITE paper) **and heard the wind. She wondered if she'd live to feel it on her face again.**

As she grew closer to the king, she heard royal banners snapping in the breeze (hold up BLUE paper also). **The king was behind heavy doors. As Esther reached the doors the wind died away** (lower WHITE paper). **The banners hung straight and still** (lower BLUE paper).

Esther raised her hand. She was afraid to knock. Then she recalled her uncle's words: "What if God made you queen for just this reason?"

She knocked (hold up YELLOW paper) **and heard the sound echo in the king's chamber. What would happen when the door opened?**

Lower the YELLOW paper.

Say: **The king wasn't angry—he welcomed Esther. And he changed his plans. He decided not to kill the Jews. The Jews were saved!**

God *did* have a special plan for Esther—and God has a special plan for you, too.

Turn to someone seated near you. Quickly pray together that God will use you—in school, at home, or at your job—to honor and serve him.

Remind everyone to use the fun ideas in the Sticky Note bulletin inserts this week.

30. Got What You Need?

The Passage: Psalm 23

The Point: God gives us all we need.

The Props: none

Quick Summary: You'll use the 23rd Psalm to help your audience discover that God gives us all we need.

Say: **A quick question: What do you need to get by?**

Turn to a neighbor and tell that person two things that you believe you need to get through the day. Things you need to survive. And just so you know, coffee isn't technically a requirement for survival.

Allow 45 seconds for sharing, then draw attention back to yourself.

Say: **I have a list here. See if it matches yours. Raise your hand if you mentioned needing a large rock? sunscreen? a fishing pole? wood?** Allow time between each question for hands to be raised.

Say: **You might have added those items if I'd mentioned that you're stranded on a deserted island far out in the ocean. With a rock, you can open coconuts. Sunscreen will keep you from baking. The fishing pole lets you catch your dinner, and wood lets you cook it.**

Psalm 23:1 says, "The Lord is my shepherd; I have all that I need." What confuses us is that we don't always _know_ what we need.

> ## For Extra Impact
> *Project a deserted beach picture where your audience can see it.*

Maybe we're not growing in our faith because we're too comfortable. God might send some challenges our way to remind us that we need him. Or perhaps we're happy where we are and God wants us to serve in another city. Losing a job might be just what we need to get us to a new place.

God gives us what we need to serve him—and that's what we should want most!

Remind everyone to use the fun ideas in the Sticky Note bulletin inserts this week.

31. Time to Trust

The Passage: Proverbs 3:5-6
The Point: Trust in the Lord always.
The Props: none
Quick Summary: Using Proverbs 3:5, you'll explain how we all need to trust the Lord—no matter what.

Say: **I'm leaving town. I have lots of houseplants, and I can't take them with me. If you'll water my plants every day for a month, I'll pay you. You'll get five cents the first day and I'll double your payment every day.**

On day two, you'll get 10 cents. Day three, it's 20 cents. Day four, it's 40 cents.

> ### For Extra Impact
> *Project a picture of a houseplant.*

Raise your hand if you want the job. It's a good deal—trust me.

Allow time for people to raise their hands.

Say: **You won't regret this. But everyone who *didn't* volunteer might. By the end of 30 days, you'll make more than 25 million dollars!**

Proverbs 3:5 says, "Trust in the Lord with all your heart, do not depend on your own understanding."

Some of you didn't trust me. You trusted your *own* understanding—and you didn't understand the full power of multiplication.

That's how we sometimes are with God: We depend on our own under-standing—we don't trust God. Turn to someone near you and discuss a time you trusted God. Allow 90 seconds for discussion, and then call attention back to yourself.

Say: **Of course, I was just kidding about the plants and the money. But God isn't kidding when he tells us to trust him. God keeps his promises. And he loves us—he always wants what's best for us. What God has planned for us is *way* better than anything we could come up with. So next time you're tempted to rely on your own understanding, remember this example. Don't miss out on what God has planned!**

Remind everyone to use the fun ideas in the Sticky Note bulletin inserts this week.

32. Two Arms!

The Passage: Isaiah 40:31

The Point: God gives us strength.

The Props: none

Quick Summary: You'll help your audience experience how God gives us strength.

Say: **Please stand. While I talk, I'd like you to hold your arms out straight to the side at shoulder height. Just make sure you don't hit anyone!**

After your audience is standing, arms extended, continue.

Say: **Does everyone know what a triathlon is? Just in case you don't, I'll explain.**

For Extra Impact

Project a picture of a runner, swimmer, or biker (or all three!).

Athletes who participate in a triathlon have to do three sports to complete a race. They have to run, swim, and race a bicycle.

The athletes run 26.2 miles, swim 2.4 miles, and bike 112 miles during the granddaddy of triathlons, the Ironman World Championship on the island of Hawaii.

By the way, keep those arms up!

During an Ironman triathlon, athletes burn a ton of calories—some estimate they burn between 7,000 and 12,000 calories. So triathlons are a good way to lose weight, though probably not the place to begin a weight-loss program. Are your arms getting tired yet?!

Of course, no serious athlete jumps into an Ironman without a heavy course of training. Daily training. Plus nutrition. And even with years of preparation, there are highly trained athletes who enter Ironman competitions and discover they simply can't complete the race.

In fact, it's true that winning isn't everything when it comes to an Ironman. Just completing the race is a huge accomplishment. Kind of like you right now—you want to do what I've asked and keep your arms up, but it's getting difficult. But if you drop out now, you wonder if the next thing I say is to go ahead and be seated—which I'm *not* saying!

Instead, do this: Move to a place where you can rest your arms on the shoulders of your neighbors. If you're at the end of a row with no neighbor in sight, go ahead and lower that stray arm. Pause.

Doesn't that feel better?

You could keep this up far longer than you could stand on your own. In that way, resting your arms on your neighbors is a bit like how God gives us strength.

Isaiah 40:31 says: "But those who trust in the Lord will find new strength. They will soar high on wings like eagles. They will run and not grow weary. They will walk and not faint."

If we trust in the Lord and lean on his strength in life, we'll find the strength we need.

And here's what you've all been waiting for: Please be seated!

Remind everyone to use the fun ideas in the Sticky Note bulletin inserts this week.

33. Stand Up, Sit Down

The Passage: Daniel 3
The Point: Choose to serve only God.
The Props: none
Quick Summary: You'll use the story of a blazing furnace to help your audience decide to serve God—and only God.

Say: **I have a few questions for you. You'll answer them by standing or sitting, so please get in a position where it's comfortable to stand and be seated again. Ready?**

Would you rather drink Coke or Pepsi? Stand if you would rather drink Coke.

Allow time for the audience to stand up and sit back down.

Say: **Would you rather run 10 miles or swim 5 miles? Stand if you'd rather run.**

Allow time for the audience to stand up and sit back down.

Say: **Would you rather get a paper cut on a finger or a toe? Stand if you'd rather get a paper cut on your toe.**

Allow time for the audience to stand up and sit back down.

Say: **Would you rather take a hot cookie pan from the oven without an oven mitt or let an ice cube melt in your hand? Stand if you'd rather deal with the hot stove.**

Allow time for the audience to stand up and sit back down.

For Extra Impact
Project a picture of a fire.

Say: **Would you rather worship a false god or be burned to death? Stand up if you would rather worship a false god.**

Allow time for the audience to stand up and sit back down.

Say: **That last one was a tough decision! Three men in the Bible, Shadrach, Meshach, and Abednego, had to answer the same question.**

Quickly summarize Daniel 3, reading verses 17-18.

Say: **Our three friends chose to serve only God. In making that decision, they risked their lives. This week, think about this question: What are you willing to risk to remain faithful to God?**

Remind everyone to use the fun ideas in the Sticky Note bulletin inserts this week.

34. First Things First

The Passage: Daniel 6
The Point: Keep God first.
The Props: none
Quick Summary: As you talk about firefighters, you'll help your audience decide to keep God first.

For Extra Impact

Project a picture of a firetruck or a firefighter.

Ask: **How many of you have ever wanted to be a firefighter?**

Say: **Good news—for the next few minutes, you can be firefighters! Your job is to put out fires. Of course, there aren't always fires to put out, so there are other things you do to stay busy around the firehouse.**

You'll divide your audience into four sections. Indicate the first section.

Here's what *you* do at the firehouse: You hang the hoses so they can dry. After a fire, the hoses have to drain so they don't grow weak. You haul the hoses up to a tower on the back of the firehouse and let them hang there.

Describe the action by raising your hands above your head like you're hanging something up. **Everyone in this section please stand. Show me how you hang those heavy hoses.** Pause. **Good job. Be seated.**

Section Two: Those of you in *this* section keep the fire engine shiny. Stand up and pretend you're waxing the fire engine like this. Make a rubbing action like you're holding a rag, waxing a vehicle. Allow time for participants to follow your directions. **Great—be seated.**

Section Three: You cook the meals for all the firefighters. Stand up and rub your tummies—like this. Demonstrate, then have participants mimic you. **Good job!**

Section Four: You keep the firehouse clean. Stand up and pretend you're sweeping a floor—like this. Demonstrate, then allow time for participants to mimic you. **Thank you.**

Pretend you've lost your place.

Say: **Let's see...hang the hoses, wax the fire engine, clean the firehouse...**

Point to the third group.

Ask: **What's your job again?**

Someone will call out "cook the meals."

Say: **No. Your *job* is to put out fires. You cook meals when you're not busy *doing* your job. The extra things you do around the firehouse aren't your first concern. If that fire alarm rings, you drop whatever you're doing and go take care of business. That goes for all you firefighters.**

It's easy not to put first things first. Sometimes we forget what's most important.

There's a guy in the Bible who didn't make that mistake—Daniel. He knew that no matter what his duties were as a royal administrator, his *first* job was serving God. That's why he kept praying to God even when the king made it against the law.

Daniel kept God first!

Think of something in your life that seems to crowd God out of first place. Then ask God to help you keep him first this week!

Remind everyone to use the fun ideas in the Sticky Note bulletin inserts this week.

35. Second Chances

The Passage: Jonah 1–3

The Point: God gives us second chances.

The Props: 3 rubber or plastic balls, trash can, 4 spoons, transparent tape, and 3 small prizes ($2 bills, gift certificates for a dozen donuts, it's up to you)

Quick Summary: You'll help your audience discover that through forgiveness, God gives us second chances.

Long before the audience arrives, tape three spoons under chairs. Make sure the chairs are in different parts of the room. Ask:

• **How many of you have gone to a professional basketball game?**

Allow time for hands to go up.

Say: **Those of you who haven't been to a game may not know about the ever-popular halftime half-court shot. Seats are selected at random, and whoever is sitting there can take a shot from half-court. If the ball goes in, the shooter wins a prize.**

Let's do that now. Feel under your chair to see if there's a spoon (hold up a sample) **taped there. If so, bring it to me. You'll get to take a shot at our basket and may win a valuable prize.**

If you don't find a spoon under your chair, check under empty chairs...There's one...do we have two? Three? Come on down!

For Extra Impact

Project a picture of a cheering crowd.

Give each contestant a ball. Have contestants throw the balls at a wastepaper basket that's at least 20 feet away. When all three have finished, say: **It seems that some** [or all] **of you missed. Tell you what—I'll give you another chance. From three feet away.**

Lead in applause when a shooter scores a basket. If a shooter misses from three feet, move the person one foot from the basket for another try.

Award each contestant a small prize, and ask contestants to be seated.

Say: **If we'd been at a professional game, our friends wouldn't have gotten a second chance. But we're here at church, and God is all *about* second chances. Good thing, too, especially for a man named Jonah.**

Read Jonah 2:2 aloud. Explain that Jonah chose to run away from a God-given task, and that he was given a second chance to do what God wanted—*after* Jonah was urped out of a large fish!

Say: **God gave Jonah a second chance, and he gives us second chances, too. We can come to him even after we've disobeyed him. We can ask for forgiveness. I'm glad God loves us enough to give us second chances, aren't you? I guess *God* deserves the cheers!**

Lead the audience in applause and cheers for God.

Remind everyone to use the fun ideas in the Sticky Note bulletin inserts this week.

New Testament

36. Welcome to the Neighborhood!

The Passage: Luke 2:1-20
The Point: God understands us.
The Props: none
Quick Summary: As you prompt your audience to yawn with you, they'll discover that God understands us.

Say: **Many studies indicate that a lack of sleep contributes to many problems in life. From not being able to stay awake while driving to doing poorly on tests and at work, there is a strong correlation between a lack of deep sleep and...**

For Extra Impact

Project a picture of someone yawning. Display the picture throughout your message.

Pause, and look at your audience. Give a loud, wide-mouthed yawn. It's contagious—your audience will largely respond with yawns. Ask:

• ***Now* how many of you think I understand about lack of sleep?**

It's easier to trust that I know how it feels being tired when I *show* that I'm tired. And a lot of you joined me!

The account of Jesus' birth is wonderful in many ways, one of which is this: God moved into the neighborhood.

True, God created the world. And he'd taken walks through Eden with Adam and Eve. But as for living here, moving into a small town with dirt roads and no running water—this was a first.

It's sometimes easy for us to say, "God doesn't understand what I'm going through. How can he—he's off in heaven."

When you find yourself feeling that God can't possibly know what it's like to have a tough teacher, or a mean boss, or too much to do, remember the words of an angel talking with frightened shepherds outside of Bethlehem: "The Savior—yes, the Messiah, the Lord—has been born today in Bethlehem, the city of David!" (Luke 2:11).

Sticky Faith

The angel was announcing good news: God had moved into the neighborhood! God knows all about us, and he knows that we need a Savior.

And that really is good news!

Remind everyone to use the fun ideas in the Sticky Note bulletin inserts this week.

37. Rate the Bait

The Passage: Luke 5:1-11

The Point: God can use us to bring others to him.

The Props: fishing pole and reel, a baggie of garlic, a baggie containing a sock, a baggie containing a gift certificate, and a small weight

Quick Summary: You'll cast a line several times to demonstrate that Go can use us all to bring others to him.

For Extra Impact

Project a picture of a person fishing.

Position yourself so you're standing in front of an aisle. As yc speak, tie the garlic bag to the fishing line.

Say: **I'm not much of a fisherman** [or woman]. **Many people a better at bringing home big fish for dinner.**

Some fishermen use rods and reels. Some fly fish. Some us nets. But they all have to figure out what bait to use and whei to look for fish.

In the Bible, Simon Peter fished for a living. Jesus saw him working his ne on the Sea of Galilee.

Let's see if this bait works. I've tied a bag of garlic to my line. If you wan to take the bait, go for it.

Cast the "bait" to the end of the aisle and reel in the bag. If someone wants th garlic, let the person grab it and reel him or her in. Give the person the bag, ar ask for a reaction. It will most likely be negative. If no one takes the bait, sa something like, "Hmm. I guess garlic isn't all that attractive as bait."

Continue talking as you tie a bag with a sock in it to the line. Cast it down different aisle if possible.

Say: **Dirty socks aren't used often as bait.** Reel it in. **Now I see why.**

Continue talking as you cut off the sock and tie the line to a bag in which you'v placed a gift certificate and enough weight to let you gently cast the bag.

Say: **Jesus gave Simon some advice: Go out to deep water and drop a ne there. Simon said they'd fished all night without any luck, but OK...he try.**

This time I'll use a gift certificate from [location] **as bait. Let's see if I get a bite.**

Cast the line and continue talking.

Say: **They did as Jesus said and caught so many fish that two boats began to sink. Peter fell at Jesus' feet, and Jesus told him that now he'd be fishing for people—not fish.**

Encourage people to take the bait—reassure them the gift certificate goes to whoever bites first.

Give the certificate away. Set the fishing pole aside. Hold up the sock.

Say: **The bait we use when "fishing for men" has to be something that draws people, not something that chases them away. And in John 13, Jesus tells his followers what it is: us.**

Read John 13:34-35 aloud.

Say: **When we love each other like Jesus loves us, we draw people to us** *and* **to Jesus. God can use** *you* **to draw people to Jesus!**

Remind everyone to use the fun ideas in the Sticky Note bulletin inserts this week.

38. Do to Others...

The Passage: Luke 6:31

The Point: Treat others the way you want to be treated.

The Props: none

Quick Summary: You'll help your audience discover God wants us to treat others the way we want to be treated as they consider how Jesus treated them.

As you ask your audience to do actions, demonstrate them yourself.

Say: **I'd like us to do something together. I'm going to ask you to close your eyes in a moment, but don't worry: I promise I don't have a water pistol up here!**

If you've ever hurt someone's feelings, please stand up.

If you've ever been unfair to someone, close your eyes.

If you've lied to someone—even once—raise your left arm.

If someone has ever helped you, raise your right arm.

If someone has ever helped you—and it cost that other person something—open your eyes.

If you've ever done any of those things to Jesus—hurt him by not obeying him, been unfair to him, or not told him the truth, please stay as you are.

Read aloud Luke 6:31.

We don't always do what Jesus says here...but Jesus does. Please be seated.

> ## For Extra Impact
>
> *Project a picture of Jesus on the cross.*

It's hard to treat others well when they hurt our feelings, are unfair, or lie to us. But we have a great example of how to live: Jesus!

The next time you're tempted to "get even" or act badly because someone else treated you unfairly, think about Jesus. We've all treated him unfairly, and he gave up his life for us! When in doubt, remember Jesus!

Remind everyone to use the fun ideas in the Sticky Note bulletin inserts this week.

39. Dinner Is Served!

The Passage: Mark 6:30-44

The Point: God does amazing things with what we give him.

The Props: one penny per person, offering plates

Quick Summary: You'll challenge your audience to put their trust in God as they put a penny in an offering plate.

Have your volunteers give each person one penny. If at your church you take an offering before you'll be speaking, instruct people *not* to place pennies in the offering; they'll need the pennies later.

Read aloud Mark 6:30-40.

> ### For Extra Impact
> *Project a close-up of a penny.*

Say: **Five thousand hungry people. Five loaves. Two fish. Not good odds for everyone getting a fish sandwich.**

But then a few people did something amazing.

Jesus did something amazing—he multiplied the food—but I'm thinking about someone else. I'm thinking about the people who *had* the loaves and fish, who could have kept quiet and enjoyed a private feast.

Instead, they gave the food to Jesus.

Think about it: They trusted that if they gave what little they had, Jesus could do something amazing with it.

And they weren't disappointed.

Read Mark 6:41-44 aloud.

Say: **Jesus can do amazing, incredible things with what we bring to him—but only if we trust him enough to give what we have to him.**

Look carefully at your penny. It's not worth much. It's not really amazing...but give it to Jesus and he can do amazing things with it.

On your penny it says "In God we trust." If that's true—if you trust God—he can do amazing things in and through you.

We'll take up an offering and put the money toward our mission fund [or whatever cause you choose]. **But more than offering pennies, think about**

this. If you're willing to trust Jesus with *you*, with the talents you have and all you own, drop your penny in the offering.

Ask ushers to do what your church normally does to collect offerings. Pray, asking God to help each person give themselves wholeheartedly to him.

Remind everyone to use the fun ideas in the Sticky Note bulletin inserts this week.

40. The Good Samaritan

The Passage: Luke 10:25-37

The Point: Your neighbor is whoever needs you.

The Props: none

Quick Summary: Audience members will use their fingers to decide how to help others with gifts of five minutes—and be "good Samaritans."

Say: **Please raise one hand in the air like this.** Demonstrate holding up a hand, palm facing your audience, fingers up. **Assuming your hand is like most hands, you have five fingers. Let's say you do.**

I'd like you to think of those fingers as minutes—five minutes.

Please lower your hands...but don't put away your fingers.

Turn to a neighbor and tell that person about a time someone helped you in five minutes or less. Maybe the person was a friend who helped you with a homework problem. Or it was a stranger who gave you directions when you were lost.

Take 30 seconds each to share your story with a neighbor. Who helped you in five minutes or less?

After a minute, draw attention back to yourself.

Say: **Here's a challenge for this coming week: Let's each help someone in need—in five minutes or less. That's all. We all have five minutes to spare *somewhere* in the week.**

Since you only get five minutes, helping someone is tricky.

First (hold up index finger), **you've got to *find* someone to help.**

Second (hold up your middle and index fingers together), **that person has to be willing to *accept* your help.**

Third (add your ring finger), **you've got to actually *help*—and that can feel risky and uncomfortable.**

> ## For Extra Impact
> *Project a picture of a hand with all five fingers raised.*

And fourth (add your little finger), **you've got to help someone *close by*—five minutes doesn't give you time to go across town.**

Here's an example of how that might look.

Read aloud Luke 10:30-36.

Say: **Notice that our Samaritan friend...**

First (hold up index finger), ***found* someone to help—a person in need.**

Second (hold up your middle and index fingers together), **that person was willing to *accept* his help.**

Third (add your ring finger), **the Samaritan actually *helped*—and that was risky and expensive.**

And fourth (add your little finger), **he helped someone *close by*.**

The Samaritan understood that his neighbor was anyone who needed him and on whom he could show mercy.

This week be a Five-Minute Good Samaritan. Look for an opportunity to spend just five minutes jumping in to help someone in need.

I mentioned not putting away your fingers because you'll need your thumb now. If you're willing to join me in looking for that five-minute opportunity, would you give me a thumbs up? Demonstrate.

Great. Now let's trust God to give us those chances!

Remind everyone to use the fun ideas in the Sticky Note bulletin inserts this week.

41. For What It's Worth

The Passage: Matthew 13:45-46

The Point: Knowing Jesus is worth everything.

The Props: offering plates, faux pearl beads in the offering plates (one pearl per person)

Quick Summary: You'll use Jesus' parable about a pearl of great price to help your audience decide if Jesus is most important in their lives.

Read aloud Matthew 13:45-46. Ask:

- **How many of you own some sort of pearl jewelry?** Ask for a show of hands.

Say: **Quite a few of us. Please keep your hands up. How many own a pearl that's worth millions and millions of dollars?** Hands will quickly be lowered.

For Extra Impact

Project a picture of a pearl or pearl necklace.

That's what the world's largest, most expensive pearl is worth. And you won't find it on a necklace—it weighs more than 14 pounds!

If you owned a jewelry store, you'd *love* having this one-of-a-kind pearl. Maybe that's how the man in Jesus' parable felt. He found a pearl that was worth everything he had—his house, his donkey, everything he owned. He sold them all so he could have that one pearl.

Turn to someone seated next to you and answer this question:

- **What's something I want so much that I'd give up everything I own to get it?**

Allow a minute for discussion, and then draw attention back to yourself.

Say: **Jesus says the pearl in this parable is the kingdom of heaven. It's a friendship with him. And that *is* something worth having. A friendship with him leads to a life of purpose, to eternal life, to heaven.**

But there's a cost: Like the man who wanted the pearl, we have to give up everything we have...and more. We have to give him *ourselves*.

To love him...serve him...obey him.

Are you willing to do that?

Give your volunteers the offering plates in which you've placed pearl beads. As you continue, have them pass the plates through the audience.

Say: **This time when the offering plate passes, take something *out*. In each plate are pearls. *Plastic* pearls, but pearls nonetheless. Take one, and hold the pearl in your hand.**

Your pearl is a reminder of a decision you need to make: Is a friendship with Jesus worth the cost? To love him...serve him...obey him? And not just today—but every day?

Keep your pearl where you'll see it often as a reminder of this question: Is Jesus the pearl of great price in *your* life?

Remind everyone to use the fun ideas in the Sticky Note bulletin inserts this week.

42. The Doctor Is In... Sorta

The Passage: Matthew 8:1-17

The Point: Jesus shows his power through healing.

The Props: one adhesive bandage per person (visit the Dollar Store)

Quick Summary: Your audience will consider why Jesus healed others as they tell stories of healing.

As people enter, have volunteers give each person an inexpensive adhesive bandage.

Say: **Please raise your hand if you've ever had a boo-boo. It can be a surgery, a broken bone, or a fall-off-your-bike-and-skin-your-knee boo-boo.**

For Extra Impact

Project a picture of an adhesive bandage.

In a moment, I'll ask that you open your adhesive bandage and place it on the site of a boo-boo, either on your skin or on your clothing covering the injury site.

You'll be talking about your boo-boo, so pick one you're comfortable discussing. Ready? Open up and put on those bandages!

Allow time. Encourage your audience to tuck wrappers in their pockets.

Say: **Turn to someone near you and tell the story of your boo-boo. How did you get hurt—and who helped you heal? You've each got 45 seconds to tell your story.**

Allow time for people to share, then draw attention back to yourself. Say: **Most of you have this in common: Someone helped you heal. A doctor, nurse, paramedic, your mom—someone was there.**

When Jesus was on the earth, he healed people's boo-boos. *Big* boo-boos like leprosy—a disease that dulls nerves and withers noses and fingers.

But Jesus didn't heal *everyone*. Not their bodies, at least.

Jesus didn't come to be a doctor. He said he came to seek and save the lost. He healed people to help us have faith and so people could see his power.

Jesus *can* be your healer, even if your boo-boo never gets better. He can make whole your friendship with God so you can be with him forever. And *that's* the best way to be healthy!

Remind everyone to use the fun ideas in the Sticky Note bulletin inserts this week.

43. The Best Gift of All

The Passage: John 3:16
The Point: God gave the best gift.
The Props: a large ball or toy, a tool, and a candy bar
Quick Summary: As you give away three gifts, you'll help your audience be receptive to another gift: God's love.

Ask: • **How many of you have received a gift you didn't like and couldn't use? Raise your hands.**

Give an example of such a gift you've received. Be sure it wasn't given to you by anyone in the audience!

Say: **But just because the gift wasn't something you wanted doesn't make it a *bad* gift. It just got to the wrong person.**

I have with me three gifts I don't want or need. But I'm sure *someone* here could use them. Someone here must want them. They're free. If you can use one of these, raise your hand—it's yours.

Hold up the toy—an inflatable ball or other large, colorful toy.

Say: **How about this? Anyone want it? You do? It's yours.** Toss the ball to the person who wants it. **See? A good gift...but not one I want.**

How about this tool? Hold it up. **It works fine, and maybe you can use it at your house. Or you're just out on your own and you need to start assembling some tools. Anyone? You—it's yours. Come up and get it.**

Again—a good gift...but not one I want. How about this candy bar? Ah, I see *lots* of people want this. Here you go. Toss the candy bar into the audience.

Open your Bible and read John 3:16 aloud.

Say: **Who here would like a gift of God's love? Raise your hands.** Pause. **I agree—this is a good gift. A *great* gift. And though not everyone has yet accepted it, this gift is offered to you today—right now. It's the best gift of all!**

Remind everyone to use the fun ideas in the Sticky Note bulletin inserts this week.

For Extra Impact

Project a picture of a wrapped gift.

44. Tough Love

The Passage: Matthew 27:32-56

The Point: Jesus shows us his love on the cross.

The Props: board, a kitten stuffed animal, hammer, large (easily visible) nails, a friend holding the stuffed animal

Quick Summary: Your audience—of cat people and dog people—will discover that Jesus' sacrifice on the cross was motivated by love.

Say: **They say there are two kinds of people in the world: cat people and dog people. Think for a moment which you are.**

Cat people, please raise your hands and meow. Pause. **Thank you.**

Dog people, raise a paw and bark. Pause. **Good job.**

I have here a kitten (take the stuffed animal from your friend). **She's a cutie, eh? You cat people all like her, and you dog people are thinking, "yuck!"**

Today we'll talk about Jesus' crucifixion. Some of you don't know much about crucifixion—being nailed to a wooden cross and left to die.

Hold up the props as you mention them.

Say: **So I brought a piece of wood...a hammer...and nails. We'll just nail this kitten to the wood so you can see how painful crucifixion is.**

Does that seem like a good idea?

Allow time for audience to respond.

Say: **Of course not—and we won't do it. If we nailed a real kitten to a board, we'd go to jail. It's cruel. It's torture. We'd *never* do that to a cute little kitten like this.**

But it *is* something that people just like us did—to Jesus.

Hand the stuffed animal back to your friend. Then read Matthew 27:50 aloud.

Say: **Notice Jesus "released" his spirit—he let it go. It wasn't taken from him. That's because every step of the**

For Extra Impact

Project a picture of an empty cross.

way through his arrest and torture, Jesus allowed it to happen. He could have stopped it at any time. He could have called down angels to stop the pain...but he didn't.

Why? Because, as it says in Luke 19:10, he came to seek and save the lost. People like us, who have done wrong things and sinned against God. We need someone to be a sacrifice for us, and Jesus chose to do that.

What kept Jesus pinned to the cross weren't the nails. It was love. Love for you...and for me. Remember that this week, especially if you're feeling alone or unloved.

Remind everyone to use the fun ideas in the Sticky Note bulletin inserts this week.

45. You Can't Keep a Good Man Down

The Passage: Matthew 28:5-7

The Point: Jesus rose from the dead.

The Props: none

Quick Summary: As they check their pulses, people in your audience will better imagine Jesus' death...and be amazed at his resurrection!

Say: **I'd like you to take a moment and check something you brought with you today. I just want to make sure it's working.**

It's your pulse.

For those of you who don't know, here's how to take your pulse. You've got two options.

Demonstrate as you quickly give directions.

One way is to place the tips of your index and middle fingers of one hand on your opposite wrist. Lay your fingers across the tendon and move your fingertips until you can feel a steady beat.

Another way is to place those fingertips just under your jaw in the groove where your neck meets your head. Just next to your windpipe.

Got it? Found your pulse? You should be able to feel it.

If you *can't* feel it...confirm with someone near you that you appear to be alive.

For Extra Impact

Project a picture of a smiling doctor.

Your doctor loves you having a nice, steady pulse, and here's why: It's a sign your heart is beating...your blood is flowing...that you're alive.

When your pulse *stops*—you're dying. And if it stops long enough—for five to ten minutes, say—you're probably dead. One to two hours? You're *definitely* dead.

So how about three days?

When Jesus died on the cross—a death confirmed by Roman soldiers and the people who prepared Jesus' body for burial—there was no pulse.

There was no pulse when he was put in a tomb. No pulse when a huge rock was shoved in front of the tomb to seal it.

But here's what an angel announced to women gathered at Jesus' empty tomb three days later. Read aloud Matthew 28:5-7.

Say: **Jesus once again had a pulse, beating strong and true. He'd come back to life! No doubt about it!**

Remind everyone to use the fun ideas in the Sticky Note bulletin inserts this week.

46. Wind and Fire

The Passage: Acts 2:1-4
The Point: The Holy Spirit transforms us.
The Props: pieces of paper (church bulletins work well)
Quick Summary: Members of your audience will help tell the story of Pentecost and consider how the Holy Spirit is transforming their lives.

Say: **Please take out a piece of paper** (a bulletin or other piece of paper distributed as audience members entered). **Before you do anything with your paper, decide if you're in Group 1 or Group 2.**

If your birth date falls on the first day of the month through the 15th— you're in Group 1. If it falls from the 16th through the 31st, you're in Group 2.

Let me see the hands of you Group 1 people.

Instruct Group 1 people to hold their paper between their hands and rub the paper—making the sound of a "mighty windstorm."

Ask to see the hands of Group 2 people. Help them practice holding their papers over their heads, gently shaking the papers to create "flames."

> ## For Extra Impact
> *Project a picture of a fire.*

Say: **Now everyone place your papers on your laps. You'll know what to do when the time comes.**

Read aloud Acts 2:1-4—dramatically—pausing after "windstorm" and "fire" so audience members can respond.

After completing verse 4, indicate that everyone should put down the papers.

Say: **Wow! Turn to someone seated near you and answer this question:**

   • **How would you react if this happened in our meeting today?**

Allow 60 seconds for discussion, then continue.

Say: **The Holy Spirit made a *dramatic* entrance, and the followers of Jesus were literally transformed. They changed at once. The Holy Spirit usually works more slowly in us—helping us know more about Jesus and love Jesus more deeply.**

Turn to your partner again and answer this question:

  • **How are *you* being changed?**

After 60 seconds, draw attention back to yourself and continue.

Say: **This week, pray for your partner. Ask God to use the Holy Spirit to transform your friend in new ways!**

Remind everyone to use the fun ideas in the Sticky Note bulletin inserts this week.

47. Jesus Gets Saul's Attention

The Passage:	Acts 9:1-19
The Point:	Jesus wants to get our attention.
The Props:	bullhorn (ask around to borrow one from an emergency service)
Quick Summary:	Help your audience see that Jesus wants to get their attention by getting their attention yourself.

Say: **Time for a test. I want to see which of three different ways to get your attention works best.**

Pull out the bullhorn. Say: **A warning to those who are wearing hearing aids: Turn them down.**

Speak a few lines through the bullhorn. Sweep the room so the power of the amplification hits everyone. Then put the bullhorn down.

Say: **That worked pretty well, but some of you who turned down your hearing aids aren't turning them up again! Let's try option two: waving my arms.**

For Extra Impact

Project a picture of someone shouting, but not in an angry way.

Signal by waving your arms for a few moments.

Say: **Some of you have already fallen asleep, so you didn't react at all. I guess a visual approach won't always work. OK: option three.**

Please tap the shoulder of the person next to you. Then point at me so they look this way. Pause as people comply.

That seems to have worked best of all.

But what if three amazing things happened all at once? You're blinded by a flash of light, a huge voice that only you can hear calls your name, and you're knocked to the floor?

That would get *my* attention! And it got Saul's attention, too! Listen to what happened.

Read Acts 9:1-9 aloud.

Say: **Jesus wanted to get Saul's attention because Jesus had important things for Saul to know...and do.**

Jesus has important things for you to know and do, too. How hard will he have to try to get *your* attention?

Remind everyone to use the fun ideas in the Sticky Note bulletin inserts this week.

48. Peter's Prison Escape

The Passage: Acts 12:6-9
The Point: God sets us free.
The Props: none
Quick Summary: As your audience helps tell the story of Peter's escape, they'll consider how God helps them, too.

Say: **It had been a difficult night for Peter.**

He'd been arrested and was chained between two guards. The next morning he would be standing trial before the king.

Let's imagine what happened to Peter next—and you'll provide the sound effects.

If you were born in January, February, or March, scratch your fingernails lightly on a book cover or other hard surface. Demonstrate. **You're making the sound of rats skittering along the floor of the cell.**

If you were born in April, May, or June, softly moan like this. Demonstrate. **That's the sound of other prisoners locked up down the hall.**

July, August, and September babies, you're the wind whistling in through cracks in the walls. Demonstrate.

October birthdays, thump a finger on something solid. That's the sound of prisoners hitting heavy wooden doors, trying to get the attention of the guards...who can't *hear* the thumping. November and December babies, because they're sound asleep, are guards snoring. Let's hear snoring.

Remember to make your noise *softly*. You'll know when to come in and when to quit making your noise by listening as I tell what happened.

For Extra Impact

Project a picture of the bars of an old jail cell.

Peter was in his cell, asleep.

Good thing, too, because he might have been scared of the *rats* skittering around. The jail was old, and the *wind* pushed through cracks in the walls. And down the hall, other prisoners *moaned*, now and then *thumping* the cell doors. They wanted food and water, and to be set free.

Suddenly an angel appeared and woke Peter. The angel told Peter to follow him. Chains fell off Peter's wrists. Peter walked out of his cell and he could no longer hear the *rats*. A door in front of Peter swung open. He was outside!

There was no longer the sound of *wind* blowing through walls. The *moaning* of the prisoners was behind him, too. And their *thumping* on cell doors stopped.

Peter walked away from the jail. A block later he couldn't even hear the *snoring* of the guards.

Peter was free! God had set him free!

Thank your sound effects experts. Say that just as God helped Peter escape from prison, he helps us, too.

Remind everyone to use the fun ideas in the Sticky Note bulletin inserts this week.

49. Love It!

The Passage:	1 Corinthians 13:4-7
The Point:	God's love draws us to him.
The Props:	none
Quick Summary:	You'll help your audience see how God's love draws us to him.

Ask your audience to stand.

Say: **I'm going to ask you to make a choice. If you choose the first thing I offer, turn a quarter turn to your right. That means you'll be looking at the wall over there.** Indicate wall to the right of your audience. **If you choose the second thing I offer, you'll take a quarter turn to the left. That means you'll be looking at the wall over there.** Indicate wall to left of your audience.

Let's practice.

> ### For Extra Impact
>
> *Project a picture of chocolate.*

If you'd rather have milk chocolate, turn right. Dark chocolate, left. Everyone turn one way or the other. Perfect! Now stay where you are and keep turning one quarter turn depending on how you answer the rest of these choices.

Get a birthday gift, turn to the right. Get a birthday cake, turn left.

Go to the doctor, turn right. Go to the dentist, turn left.

Eat a pizza, turn right. Eat a salad, turn left.

Play baseball, turn right. Play soccer, turn left.

Mow the grass, turn right. Rake leaves, turn left.

Grow an inch taller, turn right. Gain 10 pounds, turn left.

Wow—we're pointing all different directions. Let's try one more.

If you'd like to feel loved, turn to the front of the room. If you don't want to feel loved, turn to the back of the room.

***That* got us all on the same page. Go ahead and be seated.**

Read 1 Corinthians 13:4-7 aloud.

Say: **Love like that is a magnet—it draws us to it. We all want it. And here's good news: We can all have it in our lives if we know God. Why? Because that's a description of God's love.**

Read 1 Corinthians 13:4-7 aloud again, this time substituting "God's love" for "love" in the passage.

Remind everyone to use the fun ideas in the Sticky Note bulletin inserts this week.

50. Super Powers

The Passage:	Galatians 5:22-23a
The Point:	The Holy Spirit empowers us to become more like Jesus.
The Props:	a fabric cape
Quick Summary:	You'll help your audience consider how the fruit of the Spirit are like super powers.

For Extra Impact

Project a cartoon superhero or the Superman logo.

Place a cape over your shoulders. A modified tablecloth will work well if you pin it in place.

Say: **When I was young, my favorite superhero was** (fill in the blank) **and here's why:** (explain quickly what superhero you most admired—and why).

I *loved* **the idea of having a super power! Turn to a neighbor and answer these questions:**

- **If you could have any super power, which one would you want?**

- **How would you use your power for good?**

Here's the sad truth: No matter how hard I wished, I wasn't faster than a speeding bullet. I couldn't swing from building to building. And the police chief never once called on me to fight crime.

But lately I've seen some super powers growing in me...though not the comic-book kind. If you know, love, and follow Jesus—there are super powers growing in you!

My web-slinging stinks, but self-control is coming easier. I can't wish myself invisible, but I'm getting better at being kind. And I may never be able to fly, but I can be faithful.

Here's why: The Holy Spirit is working in my life to empower me to become more like Jesus.

Read aloud Galatians 5:22-23a.

Say: **That's what happens when we've given ourselves to Jesus. The Holy Spirit works in us to help us be more like him. To care about what he cares about. To grow up in our faith.**

And I don't know about you, but I want those "super powers." The power comes from God to change us, but it's super to be changed!

Take off your cape.

And another good thing: None of these things (read Galatians 5:22-23a) **requires that I wear a cape!**

Remind everyone to use the fun ideas in the Sticky Note bulletin inserts this week.

51. Don't Worry...Pray!

The Passage: Philippians 4:6-7
The Point: Prayer gives us peace.
The Props: rough pebbles (available at landscaping and home improvement stores)
Quick Summary: You'll help your audience discover that through prayer God gives us peace.

As people enter, have volunteers give each person a rough pebble or small stone.

Say: **How many of you have heard of "worry stones"? They're smooth stones with a thumb-sized indentation on one side. The idea is if you rub the stone when you're worried, you'll feel better.**

I'll admit it: I worry sometimes. Lately I've been worried about (name a concern you've had that is appropriate to share).

What about you? Turn to a neighbor and discuss:

   • **What's something that's worrying you today?**

You'll have 30 seconds each. I'll let you know when 60 seconds have passed.

After you've drawn attention back to yourself, ask your audience to take out the pebbles they received when they arrived.

Say: **These aren't worry stones. They aren't smooth—because our lives aren't always smooth. There are things that cause us to worry. Bullies. Sickness. Money problems.**

These are Prayer Reminder Stones. In a few moments, I'll ask you to put your stone in a pocket so you can carry it with you as a reminder to pray when you feel worried.

Just rubbing a worry stone won't help you—but when you pray, God listens. And he *can* help you!

Read aloud Philippians 4:6-7.

Say: **Hold your Prayer Reminder Stones and silently pray for the person who shared a worry with you. Ask God to help solve that worry-causing problem and to give your friend peace.**

I'll close our prayer time. Let's pray now.

After 20 or 30 seconds, pray: **Thank you for caring about us and our concerns, God. Please give us peace! In Jesus' name, amen.**

Remind everyone to use the fun ideas in the Sticky Note bulletin inserts this week.

52. Follow Jesus

The Passage: 1 Peter 2:21

The Point: Following Jesus is best.

The Props: candle and matches

Quick Summary: You'll help your audience members understand that following Jesus is the best thing to do.

Light a candle and place it where your audience can see it. Ask:

For Extra Impact

Project a picture of a flame.

• **What would we want to do if this flame suddenly spread, and we were in a burning building?**

Our goal would be to get everyone out safely.

We've not had a fire drill in a long time (ever?) **and won't have one now—but let me point out the exits from this room.** Do so.

If there *were* a fire—and there's not—I'd ask you to leave through the nearest exit. I'd ask you to leave behind everything you brought with you today. The time you spend gathering up your stuff might cost someone else his or her life.

Notice that to meet our goal—getting everyone out safely—would cost some of you nothing. Others would pay dearly.

You'd pay because tucked in the purse you leave behind is your paycheck. Or your family Bible. Some of you might even have to leave behind your lattes!

Turn to a neighbor and discuss:

• **What would it cost you to escape the fire? Would it be worth it?**

Allow 60 seconds, and then draw attention back to yourself.

Say: **It's easy to put possessions in perspective when our lives are at stake. You'll miss that purse with the car keys and wallet in it, but you want to stay alive and help your neighbors stay alive, too.**

Achieving our goal of getting us all out is worth it...even if it's costly for some of us.

God has a goal, too, and he wants to meet it.

Read 1 Peter 2:21 aloud.

Say: **God wants us to follow him and do good things for him, no matter what the cost. As his followers, he'll help meet that goal.**

He may ask some of us to be faithful followers as we move through an easy life. He may ask some of us to be faithful through tougher times. We won't all pay the same price to be faithful, just like we wouldn't all pay the same amount to get out of a burning room. But no matter how much it costs us to be faithful to God and to follow Jesus, it's worth it!

Remind everyone to use the fun ideas in the Sticky Note bulletin inserts this week.

For more **amazing resources**

visit us at
group.com...

...*or call us at*
1-800-447-1070

Group
Incredible things will happen®